KU-786-493

The
PREMENSTRUAL
SYNDROME
and
PROGESTERONE
THERAPY

The PREMENSTRUAL SYNDROME and PROGESTERONE THERAPY

Katharina Dalton M.R.C.G.P.

THE BRITISH SCHOOL OF OSTEOPATHY
1-4 SUFFOLK STREET, LONDON SW1Y 4HG
TEL: 01-930 9254-8

WILLIAM HEINEMANN MEDICAL BOOKS LTD.
London

YEAR BOOK MEDICAL PUBLISHERS INC.
Chicago

LSO MMK JGHG

First published 1977

(C) Katharina Dalton 1977

(U.K.) ISBN 0 433 07091 9

Distributed in Continental North, South
and Central America, Puerto Rico,
Hawaii and the Philippines by
Year Book Medical Publishers, Inc.

(U.S.A.) ISBN 0-8151-2265-9
Library of Congress Catalog Card Number: 77-84329

Printed in Great Britain by
The Camelot Press Ltd, Southampton

Contents

Preface

In writing this book I have kept four clear aims in mind:

1. To bring within a small volume all that is known, today, about the premenstrual syndrome and its relationship to progesterone.

2. To clarify the differences between progesterone and progestogens and ensure a clear understanding of the basis for progesterone treatment. Also to provide full details of the treatment and management of those disorders which respond readily to progesterone.

3. To provide a practical handbook for the general practitioner, half of whose women patients are potential sufferers from the disease, and to enable physicians, psychiatrists, endocrinologists and others to recognise the syndrome when it occurs within their speciality and to understand its treatment. It is hoped that it will also be of value to social workers, health visitors and medical auxiliaries, enabling them to diagnose and refer women sufferers for treatment.

4. To provide a handy book of reference for all who are concerned with the well-being of women. For this purpose each chapter is complete in itself, even though this incurs a certain amount of repetition and cross reference.

References have been kept to a minimum, but for those who wish to go more fully into the subject or seek for further enlightenment on any specific detail, a list of the author's publications has been provided which deal specifically with the different aspects of the subject.

The somatic components of the premenstrual syndrome and the value of progesterone in the treatment of premenstrual migraine were first recognised by Dr. Raymond Greene, who also accepted clinical responsibility when I treated my first cases of premenstrual asthma, epilepsy and rhinitis with progesterone. In those days we believed that the premenstrual syndrome was a rare condition, but we know now that it is the world's commonest, and probably the oldest, disease. Since those early days a considerable number of research workers have concentrated on the psychological aspects and hardly any attention has been given to the much more important somatic and hormonal aspects.

I take this opportunity of acknowledging how much Dr. Raymond Greene has contributed to my understanding of this subject, and to thank him for all his guidance and encouragement. I have, indeed, been fortunate in having so many able people from professors to medical students who have contributed much by their criticism and stimulating discussions, particular mention must be made of Dr. Christine Moore, Dr. Gwyneth Sampson and Dr. Sheila Handel who have all read the manuscript. My grateful thanks are extended to them all, especially my severest critics Dr. Maureen Dalton and Dr. Michael Dalton, and also to those most able typists Anita Dalton and Wendy Holton who have untiringly typed and re-typed the manuscript and to Jean Mann who traced the hospital records. Finally, I must acknowledge my own indebtedness, and also that of all who read this book, to my husband, the Rev. Tom E. Dalton, and thank him for the many hours he has spent struggling with my nearly incomprehensible notes and often diffuse thoughts and translated them into very readable English.

Katharina Dalton
1977

CHAPTER ONE

Introduction

Asthma, herpes, tonsillitis, acne, baby battering, epilepsy and alcoholic bouts may appear to have little in common. Nevertheless, in those cases in which there are regular recurrences during the premenstruum or menstruation, these symptoms all come within the classification of the Premenstrual Syndrome and will respond to progesterone therapy. The common factor in these apparently unrelated symptoms is their recurrence, always at the same time, in each menstrual cycle.

To appreciate why such a variety of symptoms should all respond to the same hormone, progesterone, we need only turn to Banting and Best's momentous discovery of insulin. Let us assume that their discovery had preceded Fehling's and Benedict's tests for the detection of glycosuria. Banting and Best would have found that insulin could cause a miraculous response in some cases of coma, a dramatic recovery in some cases of emaciation, perpetual fatigue and polyuria, and a marked improvement in some cases of carbuncles and peripheral neuritis. It was the use of Fehling's and Benedict's tests that enabled them to find a common factor in all these different symptoms, namely the presence of glycosuria.

In the premenstrual syndrome there is a common factor, it is the cyclical recurrence of symptoms with each menstrual cycle. Unfortunately there is no test to assist the diagnosis of the premenstrual syndrome or, indeed, of progesterone deficiency. The recognition of this syndrome must depend upon the perception of the patient or of her doctor, and the confirmation of the cyclical recurrence on a menstrual chart.

It is now 30 years since progesterone was successfully used in the treatment of the premenstrual syndrome. Today with a greater understanding of the hormonal basis of the disease, progesterone is still the specific treatment although the method of administration has been transformed as a result of the appreciation that progesterone is adequately absorbed by the rectal and vaginal routes.

Confusion among doctors regarding the differences between progesterone and progestogens led to incorrect treatment, and false conclusions were drawn from the failure to relieve the somatic symptoms.

However, once the correct treatment has been started with the natural hormone progesterone the results are quite dramatic. It is unfortunate that today there is only a handful of doctors in Great Britain who are able and ready to diagnose the premenstrual syndrome and treat it with progesterone. On the other hand there is a very real likelihood that the general public, and especially those who suffer from the syndrome, will have a fuller understanding of the illness and its treatment before many of the doctors. In this situation it is essential that a handy textbook should be available for the medical profession.

When progesterone was first isolated in 1934 its prime function was recognised as the proliferation of the endometrium and the maintenance of pregnancy. The profession used it eagerly for the treatment of severe pre-eclamptic toxaemia, threatened and habitual abortion, albeit in inadequate doses and unselectively. The fact that progesterone is species specific provides a stumbling block to the full understanding of the function of progesterone in menstruation and pregnancy. It should be mentioned here that pre-eclamptic toxaemia is also species specific and does not occur in other mammals. It is time for reassessment to be made of the part played by progesterone not only in the disorders of menstruation, but also in the maintenance of pregnancy. This book goes part of the way towards such a reassessment but its main purpose is to ensure a full understanding of the premenstrual syndrome and its treatment with progesterone.

CHAPTER TWO

Definition and Diagnosis

DEFINITION

The premenstrual syndrome covers a wide variety of symptoms which regularly recur in the same phase of each menstrual cycle, followed by a symptom-free phase in each cycle.

There are three common patterns of the timing of symptoms all of which come within the definition of the premenstrual syndrome. First, those which occur during the late premenstruum (Pattern A, Fig. 2.1); secondly those occurring at ovulation, resolving spontaneously within a day or two and reappearing during the premenstruum (Pattern B); and thirdly those with symptoms at ovulation, which gradually increase in severity throughout the entire luteal phase (Pattern C). Termination of symptoms may occur abruptly with the onset of the full menstrual flow, or even a day earlier, or gradually resolve during menstruation. Although there are many variations the same type of time pattern tends to recur in any one individual with each menstrual cycle.

The term *"premenstrual syndrome"* was chosen at a time when it was not realised that symptoms can occur at menstruation and ovulation, therefore the emphasis on "premenstrual" could result in a failure to recognise the syndrome when the symptoms occur regularly in other phases of the menstrual cycle. Nor can they rightly be called "premenstrual" when they occur at the times of missed menstruation at the menopause, or when they occur after hysterectomy or oophorectomy.

The words *"premenstrual tension"* cover only the psychological symptoms, depression, lethargy and irritability. To use them when the tension is overshadowed by more serious somatic symptoms such as asthma, epilepsy or migraine, confuses the diagnosis. The term *"premenstrual syndrome"*, however, includes both the psychological and the somatic symptoms.

When it was realised that the recurring symptoms were at their peak during the last four days of the premenstruum and the first four days of menstruation it became necessary to find the right word to cover these vital eight days. The term *"paramenstruum"* covers these two phases of the menstrual cycle. Various surveys have shown that about half of such events as accidents, suicides, and emergency hospital admissions occur during the paramenstruum (Chapter 19).

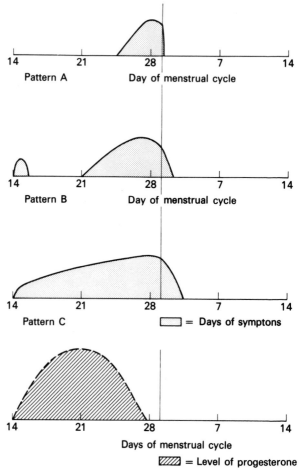

Fig. 2.1   Common patterns of timing of symptoms.

In order to study the significance of the hormonal changes during the menstrual cycle it is important to divide it into phases of hormonal activity. This fits neatly into seven, four-day phases, each phase having different levels of oestrogen and progesterone (Table 2.1).

Table 2.1

Seven four-day Phases of the Menstrual Cycle

Days	Phase	Oestrogen	Progesterone
1– 4	Menstruation	Low	Absent
5– 8	Early postmenstruum	Rising	Absent
9–12	Late postmenstruum	High	Absent
13–16	Ovulation	Falling	Low
17–20	Early luteal	Rising	Rising
21–24	Late luteal	High	High
25–28	Premenstruum	Falling	Falling

In some of the earlier work on the influence of menstruation, the menstrual cycle was arbitrarily divided into four phases, each of one week. This was a convenient division, but unfortunately it obscured the influence of the changing hormonal pattern with the result that during the premenstrual week the low incidence of events on Days 22–24 was offset by the high incidence of events during Days 25–28, likewise during the menstrual week the high incidence of events during Days 1–4 was offset by the low incidence on Days 5–7. The use of the seven-phase division clarifies the true hormonal picture.

The importance of using the seven phases of the menstrual cycle for studying the effect of the fluctuation of menstrual hormones is demonstrated in a survey into attempted suicide by Tonks and his colleagues.[3] They divided the menstrual cycle into four weeks and found that 21 of 95 attempts were made during the menstrual week and 35 attempts during the premenstrual week. Thus 56 attempts were made during the menstrual and premenstrual weeks compared with an expected 47·5 attempts had there been an even distribution. When the menstrual cycle is divided into seven phases it is seen that 39 attempts were made during the paramenstruum compared with 27·1 attempts on an even distribution, a significant difference ($P = <0.005$). In Fig. 2.2 Tonk's distribution of parasuicides is shown divided into four weeks, and below is the same distribution divided into the seven hormonal phases, which is used in most sociological studies (Chapter 19).

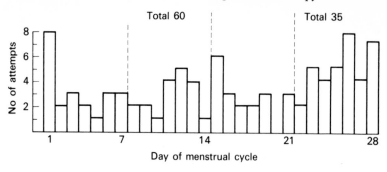

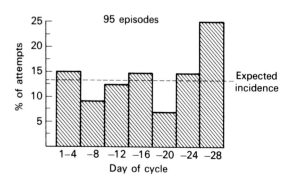

Fig. 2.2   Number of suicidal attempts in relation to the menstrual cycle. (From Tonks, C. M., Rack, P. H. and Rose, M. J. (1968), *J. Psychosom. Res.*, **2**, 319.)

DIAGNOSIS

The premenstrual syndrome is probably the only disease which, for diagnosis, does *NOT* depend upon the *TYPE* of symptoms. It is the time relationship of symptoms to menstruation that provides the diagnosis. It becomes obvious that accuracy in recording is essential for correct diagnosis. It must not be forgotten that the twenty-eight-day menstrual cycle is not a natural one, but is the average of all menstrual cycles, long and short. However, the artificial cycle produced by the oral contraceptive pill is precisely 28 days. Among non-Pill taking women a cycle length of 21 to 35 days is normal. These cycles are regarded as regular if the length does not vary by more than four days from cycle to cycle. Few women can state precisely the date of their next menstruation, and it is more usual for them to say – "This coming weekend" or "Early next week".

The only positive method of diagnosis available today, and it is the best, is the simple and inexpensive method of recording the dates of menstruation and of the symptoms on a menstrual or frequency chart such as is shown in Fig. 2.3.

	Jan.	Feb.	Mar.	Apr.	May	Jun.	Jul.	Aug.	Sep.	Oct.	Nov.	Dec.
1								M	M			
2								M				
3								M				
4							M	M				
5							M					
6						M	M					
7						M	M					
8						M						
9					M	M						
10					M							
11				M	M							
12				M	M							
13				M								
14		M	M	M								
15		M	M									
16		M	M									
17	M	M	M									
18	M											
19	M											M
20	M											M
21											M	M
22											M	M
23											M	
24										M	M	
25										M		
26									M	M		
27									M	M		
28									M			
29								M	M			
30								M				
31								M				
Total												

M = Menstruation

Fig. 2.3 Chart showing "perfect" cycle of 28 days and four days' duration.

This type of chart has stood the test of time and has much to commend it. A supply can be obtained from Drug and Therapeutics Bulletin, Consumers Association, London, W.C.2.

The menstrual chart shows at a glance the length of the menstrual cycle, duration of loss, regularity or irregularity of menstruation, the presence of ovulatory bleeding or irregular intermenstrual bleeding, and makes possible a positive diagnosis of the premenstrual syndrome. The simplicity of recording ensures the patient's co-operation (Fig. 2.4).

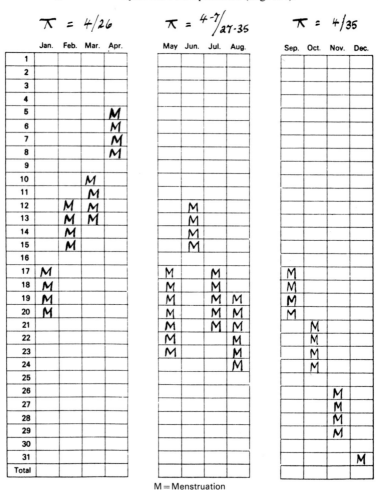

Fig. 2.4   Chart showing variations of the menstrual cycle.

The patient marks each day of menstruation by an "M" in the appropriate square on the chart. An "X" may be used for any symptom (e.g. weeping, tantrums, quarrels, depression, asthma, vertigo, migraine, headache, backache, epileptic fits, pain, herpes, rhinitis or urticaria). Such a code enlists the patient's full co-operation; few women want to keep an open record of their tantrums. Where there are many symptoms, other letters may be added, e.g. "H" for headache and "B" for backache; capitals for severe attacks, small letters for mild ones. The response to any treatment is clearly visible (Fig. 2.5).

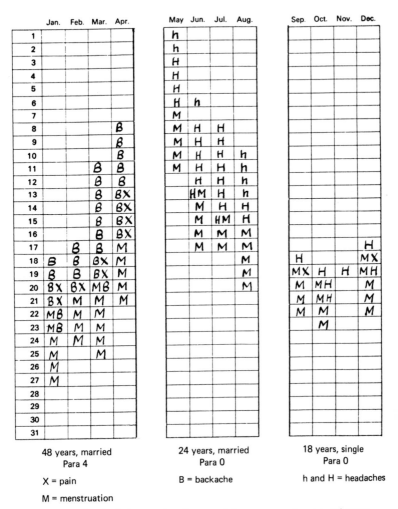

Fig. 2.5 Typical charts of sufferers of the premenstrual syndrome.

If the "M"s on the chart tend to cluster in a horizontal line, the length of cycle is 30–31 days (allowing for the varying lengths of calendar months). If the line of "M"s runs obliquely upwards, the cycle is shorter; if the "M"s slant downwards, it is longer. The time of the expected menstruation can be predicted by extending the line of "M"s into the next month (Fig. 2.4).

In the premenstrual syndrome symptoms cluster about the time of menstruation, either before or during, with the remaining days free from all symptoms. Ovulatory attacks usually stand out clearly at mid-cycle, but occasionally symptoms may begin at ovulation and continue until menstruation, with only the postmenstruum free of symptoms.

Some women, notably those with an intra-uterine device, may have only slight bleeding for a few days before the onset of full menstruation, and special symbols should be used to denote this, often with an "S" for spotting or slight bleeding.

Chronic diseases are sometimes exacerbated at the time of menstruation, e.g. rheumatoid arthritis, Crohn's disease, the pyrexia of pulmonary tuberculosis, or the oedema of cardiac disease. By charting their exacerbations, patients can allay the fear that their general condition is deteriorating.

At the menopause the chart may show that headaches, vertigo, backache or other symptoms still occur at the times of missed menstruation. Menstruation after a prolonged gap tends to occur at about the time of expected menstruation, as forecast by continuing the line of "M"s across the chart. These charts can also be given to the husband for him to chart the days when he feels his wife is being unreasonable or unduly depressed. They can be used in respect of a child with recurrent colds or psychosomatic symptoms to see whether they correlate with the mother's menstruation. The charts are particularly useful for recording recurrent symptoms in pre-pubertal girls, postmenopausal women and those who have had a hysterectomy, cyclical attacks of symptoms may occur and the response to treatment is just as good as if menstruation was occurring. Symptoms limited to the postmenstruum are extremely rare and any patient claiming such a relationship to menstruation should be asked to keep a careful record for a few months before accepting such a claim. Often symptoms occurring after the periods are in fact ovulatory attacks, i.e. they occur a week after the end of menstruation.

Prior to treatment it is essential to obtain a good record of the individual's normal duration of loss and length of cycle. Hormones may either lengthen or shorten the cycle and the duration of loss, and without knowledge of the patient's norm it is difficult to distinguish any alteration in an individual patient. The difference is often quite surprising between the actual cycle and that stated by the patient at her first interview; most women incorrectly claim to have a regular cycle of 28 days.

Not all women who have episodic symptoms have them in relation to menstruation, there may be many other unrecognised factors. Attacks may be on one particular day of the week or at weekends. If this is suspected the information on the chart may be transposed to the days of the week as in Fig. 2.6.

The chart in Fig. 2.6 was from a 27-year-old secretary who had migraine attacks at fortnightly intervals, originally on Tuesdays but later on Thursdays. It was only by keeping a careful record that it became obvious that these migraine attacks were unrelated to menstruation, which occurred at an interval of 29–30 days. Further questioning as to what Tuesday activity had been transferred to Thursday, revealed that on Tuesdays she went direct to her hairdresser from work having only had a snack lunch. The migraine developed on her way home at about 20.00 hours. When her favourite hairdresser changed her late night to Thursdays the patient changed her appointment to that day. In her case the migraine attacks were due to fasting and not related to menstruation.

Another example was seen in a Cypriot housewife with an unmanageable child. She was referred with numerous psychosomatic symptoms, including abdominal pain, possibly at mid-cycle. When she returned after a month, it was possible after examining the chart to guess that her husband worked late on Saturday, but had his half-day on Thursday. Pains were absent when father was at home to accept responsibility for the naughty boy on Thursday and Sunday, but pains increased in severity when the mother had to cope alone with the child all day on Saturday and put him to bed.

Monthly attacks of symptoms unrelated to menstruation may be noted among those in stockbrokers, accountancy and wages offices where the stress of work at the end of each month may precipitate symptoms. In other cases a monthly social or even the husband's monthly sales conference may be the root cause.

The fact that symptoms always occur on one day of the week are not always quite so easily explained. An adopted 16-year-old girl had asthmatic attacks on Monday, not in every week, but always on that day. The psychiatrist explained this by the patient being at home at weekends and being reminded of her adoption. The allergist's explanation was her allergy to house dust, for at weekends she would clean out her room. A three-month calendar revealed that she had an unusually precise menstrual cycle of 28 days, although she was not on oral contraceptives, and attacks were occurring on the 28th day, and occasionally on the 14th day; her

Sunday   —
Monday   —
Tuesday   1111
Wednesday   —
Thursday   111111
Friday   —
Saturday   —

	Jan.	Feb.	Mar.	Apr.	May	Jun.	Jul.	Aug.	Sep.	Oct.	Nov.	Dec.
1						H						
2												
3												
4												
5												
6												
7												
8										H		
9									H			
10												
11												
12							H					
13							H					
14												
15						H						
16												
17												
18												
19						M						
20						M	M					
21						M	M	M				
22							M	M				
23								MH				
24												
25												
26												
27							H					
28												
29						H	H					
30												
31												
Total												

H = migraine   M = menstruation

Fig. 2.6   Chart showing attacks at fortnightly intervals. (From *J. Roy. Coll. Gen. Pract.* (1973).)

menstruation started on Tuesdays. She responded to progesterone therapy.

Patients can often assist with past dates by searching the pages of their diaries and producing definite evidence of the dates of previous attacks and of menstruation; these are easily recalled if they coincide with an important event like Christmas, weddings and holidays. On one occasion when the author was trying to arrange a social gathering, the secretary of the society produced her diary to see if a proposed date was suitable. "No," she declared, "I'll be having a migraine on that day." Some patients make a note of forthcoming attacks.

If a patient has the notes of the dates of menstruation, but not of the times of symptoms, it may be possible to obtain these by noting absences on the work sheet, dates of attendances at the sickbay, surgery or hospital attendances. In one case the crime sheet showed a 45-year-old woman charged with "drunk and disorderly conduct" on the first or second day of menstruation on four consecutive occasions.

In the premenstrual syndrome a period free from symptoms occurs at the same phase of each cycle. When attacks occur at ovulation they are usually also accompanied by premenstrual attacks, and they may merge into one prolonged attack with exacerbations, but with a symptom-free phase during the postmenstruum. One unfortunate Irish woman complained, "I only feel well when I'm poorly."

Recording the dates of menstruation and of symptoms takes time, but careful history taking may reveal a few diagnostic pointers which can be of value in deciding whether and when to begin treatment.

BIOCHEMICAL ASSAYS

Unfortunately there are no biochemical or other tests that can compare with a well-completed menstrual chart for confirming the diagnosis of premenstrual syndrome. While there is much to suggest that progesterone deficiency,[2, 4] either absolute or relative, or through a failure in the hypothalmic feed-back mechanism, plays a part in the aetiology of this syndrome, there is little evidence that costly, isolated radioimmunoassays of plasma progesterone levels during the luteal phase or the premenstruum are helpful. Progesterone is secreted episodically in 20-minute spurts, so single blood samples are only of very limited value in assessing the competence of a patient's hypothalamic-pituitary-ovarian pathways.[6] There is, however, a need for continued research with frequent hormonal estimations taken over several menstrual cycles to assist in our further understanding of the premenstrual syndrome.

If it is proposed to carry out progesterone plasma estimations, these are best performed 7 and 11 days after the temperature rise of ovulation, when they should reflect the peak level on day 21 compared with the drop on day 25. Even if these tests are within normal limits, the presence of the premenstrual syndrome is not excluded. Similarly, the 24-hour collection of urine for the estimation of pregnanediol, the major metabolic reduction product of progesterone, is unreliable. Although urine is the main pathway for the excretion of progesterone metabolites, a variable proportion is also excreted via the bile faeces, expired air and the skin.

Basal Temperature Chart

Deficiency of progesterone may be shown up on a basal temperature chart, where the normal rise occurs at ovulation, but then the temperature falls showing a deficient luteal phase. It has been estimated that among a group of apparently normal women 5% show anovular cycles and 12·5% a defective luteal phase[2] (Fig. 2.7). A normal menstrual cycle has been defined as one showing all the following features:[1]

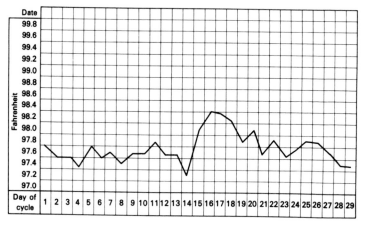

Fig. 2.7   Basal temperature graph showing defective luteal phase.

1. Mid-cycle peak of luteinising hormone.
2. Luteal phase lasting 12–16 days.
3. Progesterone values greater than 5 ng/ml 5–8 days after the surge of luteinising hormone.

Administration of progesterone during the second half of the cycle produces a raised basal temperature. However, it should be stressed that the premenstrual syndrome does not depend on ovulation, indeed it can occur at times of missed menstruation, at the menopause and after oophorectomy.

PROLACTIN ESTIMATION

Radioimmunoassays of prolactin are now available, and have been found to be raised in some women with premenstrual syndrome. The exact significance of hyperprolactinaemia in the premenstrual syndrome is not yet fully understood. Initially it was hoped that women with premenstrual syndrome and raised prolactin levels would respond well to bromocriptine. No correlation has yet been found between the levels of prolactin in women with the premenstrual syndrome and their response to treatment with either bromocriptine or progesterone. In a recent series of 67 patients with severe premenstrual syndrome 31% were found to have hyper-prolactinaemia, but only a third responded to bromocriptine, and just as many who had normal levels also showed some benefit.

ATTACK FORMS

Some of the acute episodes, which may occur in this syndrome, appear to result from transient hypoglycaemia, common during the premenstruum. If this is suspected the use of an attack form as in Fig. 2.8 provides valuable information.

It can be used in cases of migraine, fainting, aggressive outburst, phobic panic attacks, epilectic fits and any symptoms having an acute onset which can be accurately timed. The patient is asked to complete an attack form immediately after each of her next three attacks, stating all that she had done, and particularly all the food she has consumed, during the 24 hours immediately preceding the attack. The forms give quick and accurate information which, if sought several days later would take much more time and would not provide the accurate information required. The questions are so phrased that they cover women who have a short cycle of 21 days or a long one of 35 days. It is surprising how frequently one meets women with acute premenstrual attacks which occur after long intervals without food.

A 22-year-old part-time teacher was referred by a psychiatrist for premenstrual weeping attacks which occurred "at all times of the day and apparently without provocation". The menstrual chart confirmed that they were occurring during the late premenstruum, while the attack forms

Name..   Date ....
                                                    Day of week ....
                                                    Time of onset...
                                                    Duration..
Day of cycle..   Days before next menstruation.......................
During the 24 hours *before* the attack:—
(1) Did you have any special worry, overwork or shock?
(2) What had you done during the day?
          Normal work?
          Unusual activity?
          Extra tired?
(3) What food had you eaten and when?
    Breakfast ....   Time..
    ....
    Mid-morning................................   Time..
    ....
    Lunch...   Time..
    ....
    Mid-afternoon................................   Time..
    ....
    Supper ....   Time..
    ....
    Evening................................   Time..
    ....
    Bedtime ....   Time..
    ....

Fig. 2.8   Attack form. (From *J. Roy. Coll. Gen. Pract.* (1973).)

showed that the attacks were preceded by several hours of fasting. The patient had noticed that she always gained weight premenstrually and so she dieted stringently at this time. When seen at 17.00 hours she had been weeping spontaneously in the waiting room, and later stated that she had only had a small helping of cereals for breakfast at 08.00 hours and an apple for lunch as she was going out to dinner with friends later. Avoiding fasting cured the weeping.

MENSTRUAL HISTORY

A normal pain-free menstruation is the most usual, indeed, the very reason many sufferers from migraine, asthma and epilepsy fail to appreciate the time relationship of attacks is because menstruation is so uneventful that its comings and goings pass unrecognised. Spasmodic dysmenorrhoea, in the form of cramping pains in the lower abdomen, possibly radiating down the inner sides of the thighs, and coinciding with the onset of menstruation is rare (Chapter 12), although this may be produced during treatment by an overdose of progesterone in a nulliparous woman. Heaviness and dragging of the lower abdomen may be present for some days before menstruation and is relieved by the menstrual flow. Symptoms are rare in those with short cycles of less than 24 days, but among those with longer cycles, e.g. over 33 days, the attacks are usually prolonged. There may be complaints of heavy loss due to the release of retained fluid during a spontaneous diuresis. Although patients are often eager to ascribe their symptoms to the menopause, it is worth remembering that sufferers from the premenstrual syndrome are those whose menstruation usually continues the longest, with their last menstruation occurring between 50 and 55 years.

EFFECT OF PREGNANCY

Sufferers usually conceive easily and most experience an exceptionally severe and prolonged attack of symptoms at the time of their first missed period. However, once the first trimester is passed the majority become free from symptoms and will recall the feeling of exceptional well-being during later pregnancy. Those whose symptoms do not disappear during later pregnancy, but in fact increase in frequency and severity, are likely to develop pre-eclampsia. The incidence of the premenstrual syndrome following pre-eclampsia is high, 78% after one pregnancy, rising to 100% after four pregnancies, where at least one pregnancy was complicated by pre-eclampsia. Thus, in history taking it is useful to ask about their state of health in early and late pregnancy, and to question the possibility of pre-eclampsia or of oedema of pregnancy (Chapter 15).

EFFECT OF CHILDBIRTH

During the puerperium there may be an unexpected attack of the usual premenstrual symptoms, e.g. migraine or asthma usually occurring about the eighth to tenth day. Puerperal depression is a common sequel, especially in those who felt exceptionally fit during the pregnancy. Childbirth often heralds the onset of the premenstrual syndrome, and many subsequently suffer from lethargy and increasing weight (Ch. 16).

THE EFFECT OF THE ORAL CONTRACEPTIVE PILL

Most patients with premenstrual syndrome have difficulty in tolerating the Pill, often they find it necessary to stop because of side effects within a few days of beginning the first course. All women should be asked how well they tolerate the Pill.

WEIGHT FLUCTUATIONS

Patients are usually aware that their weight is rarely stable. They are apt to give their weight as "within half a stone", and may explain how they are "always going up or down" and are "never the same weight two days running". They may even have noticed a diurnal variation of 0·5–1·5 kg for which they are apt to lay the blame on inaccurate weighing scales. An increase in weight is common at ovulation, and this may lead to the erroneous belief that changes in weight are not related to menstruation; it is only if the weight is regularly charted that a rhythm is noticed. Again, patients may complain that reducing diets are no good for them, describing how their weight increased by 0·5–1·5 kg after a week's painful dieting during the premenstruum. If weight reduction is attempted on these patients fluid and salt restriction may be of greater importance than calorie limitation.

In patients, who do not possess weighing scales, useful measurements of premenstrual bloatedness can be taken each night at the level of the umbilicus while standing, and a written record kept. The weight fluctuations are decreased if the patient has been lying horizontal for two or more hours during the day, and this should be noted on the record.

FLUID INTAKE

Some women feel bloated after drinking too much fluid, and prefer to drink a cup of strong coffee in which the caffeine acts as a diuretic.

EFFECT OF PROLONGED STANDING

Although sufferers are often energetic and healthy women, nevertheless it is just these women who have difficulty in standing upright for a long time. They may describe how "all the strength drains away", and they may feel faint or actually lose consciousness. This symptom is probably related to the development of oedema in the ankles and legs. Many soon learn that the situation is eased by leaning against something, and one patient described how she recognised co-sufferers as they edged their way to lean against the walls at cocktail parties.

EFFECT OF STRESS

Some patients are aware that their symptoms are increased at times of stress, and whenever a patient complains of a particularly severe attack it is always worth while asking if they can account for this increased severity. Examination of the dates of previous hospital admissions can sometimes be explained by patients themselves, as having coincided with a particularly worrying period of their life, e.g. domestic crises, legal problems, quarrelling neighbours.

References

1. Abraham, G. E., Odell, W. D., Swerdloff, R. S., and Hopper, K. (1972), *J. Clin. Endocrin. Met.,* **34**, 312–318.
2. Backstrom, T., and Carstensen, H. (1974), *J. Steroid Biochem.* **5**, 257.
3. Lenton, E., and Cooke, I. D. (1974), *Clinics Obstet. Gynaec., 1,* **1**, 313–344.
4. Munday, M. (1977), *Curr. Med. Res. Opin.,* 4, Suppl. **4**, 19.
5. Tonks, C. M., Rack, P. H., and Rose, M. J. (1968), *J. Psychosom. Res.,* **2**, 319–323.
6. West, C. D., Mahajan, D. K., Chaure, V. J., Nabors, C. J., and Tyler, F. H. (1973), *J. Clin. Endocrin. Met.,* **36**, 1230–1236.

CHAPTER THREE

Symptomatology

The diagnosis of the premenstrual syndrome depends on the time relationship of symptoms to menstruation, NOT on specific symptoms. Symptoms which can occur in this syndrome are of extraordinary diversity and include many of the commonest symptoms of each medical speciality (Table 3.1). It would seem that no tissues in the body are exempt from the cyclical changes of the menstrual cycle, and all can be affected

Table 3.1

Common Symptoms of the Premenstrual Syndrome

Psychological	Tension
	Depression
	Irritability
	Lethargy
Neurological	Migraine
	Epilepsy
	Syncope
Dermatological	Acne
	Herpes
	Urticaria
Respiratory	Asthma
	Rhinitis
Orthopaedic	Joint pains
	Backache
Ophthalmological	Glaucoma
	Conjunctivitis
	Styes
Otolaryngorhinological	Sinusitis
	Sore throats

by cyclical premenstrual symptoms or exacerbations of chronic disorders.

The psychological symptoms of premenstrual tension, with its depression, irritability and lethargy, are undoubtedly the commonest and it is possible that tension is always present, even if overshadowed by more serious presenting symptoms, such as asthma, epilepsy or migraine. A housewife presented with a minor herpes on her upper lip and added "I can't put up with these much longer, they make me feel so ill, I feel exhausted and have headaches for two days before, and I am ready to take my life." The visible symptom was covering up the invisible distress of the premenstrual syndrome.

POLYSYMPTOMATIC

One characteristic is the tendency for the patient to be polysymptomatic with an increasing accumulation of symptoms which reach a crescendo on the final day of the premenstruum. Frequent combinations are tension, headache and mastitis, or depression, backache and nausea. The symptoms do not necessarily all start at the same time. A woman may wake up one morning feeling the world is against her, tired, yet making an effort to get up and carry on with her normal routine. A couple of days later she may be conscious of painfully engorged breasts, and realise that she is irritable with the children. Gradually she develops a headache, which increases in severity over the next 12 or 24 hours until she is prostrated with photophobia, vomiting and with a throbbing hemicranial headache. With the onset of menstruation her migraine eases and so do her other symptoms.

The Timing of Symptoms

The common time-patterns of symptoms are shown in Fig. 2.1. Frequently symptoms have been present for a few days before they become incapacitating. Analysis of absenteeism due to sickness among women employees showed that it occurred predominantly during the last four days of the premenstruum and the first four days of menstruation. In many women there is often a day or two of slight menstrual bleeding before the onset of the full menstrual flow, and it is not uncommon, among these women, to find symptoms persisting through the first few days of the cycle.

Onset of Symptoms

Symptoms often start abruptly on waking in the morning. The woman may state that she "feels different" or that she "knows the kind of day it'll be". There is then an increase in severity and possibly an increase in the number of different symptoms, such as headache, backache, oedema, until they reach a crescendo on about Day 1, or more rarely Day 28. On the other hand onset may be preceded by a day of restless activity or hypermania which is later blamed for the onset of the attack. The husband has often been heard to say, "She does too much and brings on her own attacks." One patient described how, "I do mountains of housework, then suddenly it all changes," and another, "I'm a bundle of restless energy until it starts."

In contrast the end of an attack is often abrupt, coinciding with the onset of the full menstrual flow, which may be described in such phrases as "a cloud lifts", "like a switch it's gone" and "suddenly my head clears and I know I will be all right".

The phase of the cycle when the patient is free from symptoms is usually during the postmenstruum.

Transition of Symptoms

Over the years there may be a gradual transition of the main symptoms, particularly when the normal course of the premenstrual syndrome has been interrupted with a pregnancy.

Premenstrual rhinitis may be gradually replaced by premenstrual asthma. Premenstrual backache, may later present as mastitis, with backache as a secondary symptom, and gradually abdominal bloatedness may be more important although engorged breasts and backache are still present.

FAMILIAL TENDENCY

While recognising the wide range of possible symptoms, there is a familial tendency for members of the same family to present with similar symptoms. Thus some families are troubled most with depression, and others by migraine, asthma or epilepsy. If one member of the family presents with a good record showing correlation of symptoms with the menstrual cycle, and the next member gives a history of similar symptoms but without any record of time relationship to the menstrual cycle there is a strong possibility that the next month's recording will confirm the diagnosis of the premenstrual syndrome. Indeed there are occasions on which, if there is a strong family history, it would be justifiable to commence treatment before a positive record is available.

EFFECT OF STRESS

As with all hormonal diseases, at times of stress the symptoms of the premenstrual syndrome are increased in severity and number. The mild and easily controlled tension or headache, otherwise relieved by a simple analgesic, may be suddenly exacerbated and additional symptoms become manifest at times of redundancy, bereavement or financial embarassment or whenever the life situation becomes intolerable.

A fortunate win at the pools was known to cure one housewife of premenstrual asthma, which later returned when she was covering up for her son's delinquency.

The influence of stress may come to light if, when taking a full medical history, a special note is made of the times of previous illnesses, particularly previous investigations of the same symptoms and later, when taking a social history, keeping these events in mind. This was illustrated in a mother of four children who attended with a good menstrual record showing premenstrual backache and headaches, which she stated had been present since the birth of her first child. She had previously attended the Neurological Clinic for investigation of her headaches at the time she moved into a new house. Four years later she attended the Orthopaedic Clinic for investigations and physiotherapy shortly after both parents had been killed in a road accident. She had her sinuses x-rayed at the same time as her husband was in hospital having a gastrectomy. Thus stress caused her chronic premenstrual symptoms to become unbearable and she demanded treatment at these times.

It must be remembered that stress can also alter the length of cycle or duration of menstrual loss, as well as increasing the severity of premenstrual symptoms, as is well known with the bride on her wedding night. This was illustrated in an analysis of the days of menstruation of 91 girls aged 16 years at a boarding school, who were all taking their "O" level examinations at the same time. Whereas an average of 16 girls were menstruating on any one day during the month of May on one day during the stress of examination week in June as many as 36 girls were menstruating (Fig. 3.1).

SITE OF SYMPTOM

The site of the predominant symptom may be localised in relation to the patient's current occupation. In 1954 during a survey into the incidence of premenstrual syndrome in the general population, part of the investigation was carried out in a light engineering factory employing some 3,000

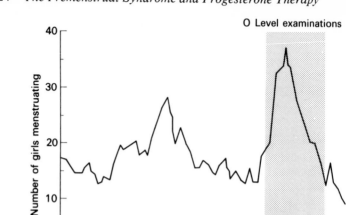

Fig. 3.1 Time of menstruation of 91 examination candidates. (From Dalton, K. (1968), *Lancet*, II, 1386.)

women. Batches of about twenty women were interviewed each day, and it was noted that on some days complaints of backache predominated, while on other days headaches were a common symptom. Then it was learnt that the women were released from one department at a time. Those complaining predominantly of premenstrual backache were employed in the packing department where the work entailed standing and lifting, while those with premenstrual headaches sat all day at a bench under strong light assembling minute parts, a task requiring a high level of concentration and visual acuity.

EXACERBATION OF CHRONIC DISEASES IN THE PREMENSTRUUM

Many chronic diseases have a premenstrual exacerbation and it is characteristically those diseases which usually improve during pregnancy, examples include rheumatoid arthritis, exogenous depression, ulcerative colitis, asthma and peptic ulcer. Deterioration in mitral stenosis as evidenced by increasing dyspnoea, haemoptysis, oedema and signs of right ventricular failure have been noted to increase during the premenstruum with marked improvement during the postmenstruum. It is because of the possibility of chronic disease being present that it must be stressed again that in the premenstrual syndrome there is always a phase free from all symptoms during the postmenstruum.

SIMILARITY OF PREMENSTRUAL SYMPTOMS TO SYMPTOMS IN PRE-ECLAMPSIA

Among women who develop pre-eclampsia 87% subsequently suffer from the premenstrual syndrome regardless of whether the premenstrual syndrome had its onset before or after the affected pregnancy. It is usual for each individual to experience the same symptoms both during the premenstruum and during the affected pregnancy. Thus one woman may be afflicted by occipital headaches and backache, and another by vertigo and paraesthesia of her hand and feet. This is shown in Fig. 3.2 giving the pattern of premenstrual and pregnancy symptoms experienced by 191

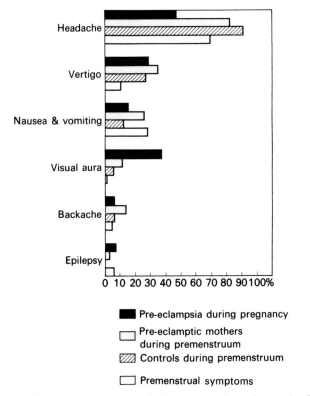

Fig. 3.2 Symptoms present during pre-eclampsia and the premenstruum.

sufferers from pre-eclampsia, compared with 169 controls and 87 women who suffered from the premenstrual syndrome, but had experienced normal pregnancies.

MECHANISMS OF SYMPTOMS

The wide diversity of symptoms which are manifested in the premenstrual syndrome appear to result from an alteration of one or more of the known functions influenced by the adrenal gland, viz:

1. Water retention
2. Potassium depletion and sodium retention
3. Hypoglycaemia
4. Allergic reactions
5. Lowered resistance to infections
6. Inflammatory reactions

Water Retention

This is responsible for such symptoms as oedema of the ankles, bloated abdomen, puffy face, engorged breasts, nasal obstruction, sinusitis, headache and eye pain. It is suggested by the oliguria and weight gain which precede an attack and the spontaneous diuresis and weight loss which mark the end of an attack. The water retention may be local or general, and only if general will it be recognised by weight gain. Only a minute increase in the amount of aqueous humour is required to cause a rise in intra-ocular pressure, an amount which is not necessarily revealed by the omnibus method of weighing the whole patient.

Localisation of water retention may be manifested in three ways:

1. Acute symptoms from localised oedema, as with migraine or epilepsy, sinus headaches, vertigo due to oedema in the labyrinth, and pruritis from subcutaneous oedema.
2. Vague symptoms resulting from widespread distribution as in fibrositis, abdominal bloating and generalised heaviness.
3. A gain in weight without any symptoms can occur, especially in the obese when the fluid is distributed in the fat and subcutaneous tissue.

In many surveys a weight gain during premenstruum has been observed to occur in those with or without symptoms and has been falsely interpreted as meaning that water retention is not a significant factor in premenstrual syndrome. To many women water retention is an important

Table 3.2

Symptomatology of the Premenstrual Syndrome

Water retention	Bloatedness
	Weight gain
	Oedema
	Backache
	Sinusitis
	Glaucoma
Sodium and potassium imbalance	Tension
	Depression
	Irritability
	Lethargy
Hypoglycaemia	Headaches
	Epilepsy
	Fainting
	Panics
	Nausea
	Exhaustion
	Aggression
Allergy	Asthma
	Rhinitis
	Urticaria
Lowered resistance to infection	Upper respiratory infections
	Tonsillitis
	Acne
	Styes
	Conjunctivitis
	Boils
	Herpes

factor, and they benefit from diuretics. However there are other factors responsible for the premenstrual symptoms in those who do not show a weight gain and such patients do not benefit from diuretics.

The actual site of the oedematous cells may vary from time to time, factors which determine their location include:

1. Anatomical. A sinus headache is more likely to occur if in addition to

engorged mucus membrane there is a deflected septum; and a closed angle at the anterior chamber of the eye can interfere with the normal outflow of intra-ocular fluid.

2. Heredity, as with a family history of epilepsy. An anatomical abnormality can also be inherited.
3. Injury. Fluid is readily attracted to a site which has recently been oedematous as a result of injury, such as a fractured wrist or ankle, and for many months there may be a tendency for premenstrual oedema to recur at the site of the old injury.
4. Infection. Following pneumonia there may be recurrent premenstrual dyspnoea for the next few months, as cells which have recently been inflamed easily become oedematous.

Potassium Depletion and Sodium Retention

It is the imbalance of potassium and sodium which is responsible for the tension symptoms of lethargy, muscle weakness, irritability and depression, and this explains why diuretics, which assist symptoms due to water retention, do not remove the tension symptoms and indeed may increase symptoms causing hypokalaemia and an increase of lethargy and irritability. At the peak of premenstrual tension one may find a low potassium level, and indeed such patients will benefit from potassium supplement to raise their potassium from the lower level of normal range, to an optimum of 4.0 to 4.3 mmol/l.

Hypoglycaemia

As long ago as 1947 Billig and Spaulding[1] noted lowered fasting blood sugar levels and lowered glucose tolerance in fourteen sufferers of the premenstrual syndrome. Transient hypoglycaemia may account for such symptoms as fainting, panic attacks, aggressive outbursts, headaches, and nausea. By obtaining a detailed history of food intake immediately prior to an attack it is possible to differentiate these cases (see page 15). It is usual to find that five or more hours have elapsed during the daytime, with a busy schedule intervening, prior to an attack. There is a natural temptation to diet and limit food intake at a time of premenstrual weight gain and abdominal bloatedness.

An unmarried mother of a 6-year-old daughter was referred by the social agencies as she had battered her child, the last two occasions were noted to be during the premenstruum. During the interview she stated that she always felt more irritable in the late afternoon when her child returned from school. Further questioning revealed that apart from her bran at breakfast she would not eat any food until tea time. During her premenstruum her glucose tolerance was lowered and hypoglycaemia occurred more readily.

Another group at risk are young teenagers, who after an early supper have an energetic evening dancing, skating or swimming, before going to bed without further food, they then rush off to work next morning with no time for breakfast. They are liable to transient attacks of premenstrual hypoglycaemia.

Reference

1. Billig, H. E., and Spaulding, C. A. (1947), *Ind. Med.*, **16**, 336.

CHAPTER FOUR

Psychological Symptoms

PREMENSTRUAL TENSION

The commonest symptom of premenstrual syndrome is tension, which is recognised as having three components, depression, irritability and lethargy. Indeed it is likely that few cases of the premenstrual syndrome are seen in which tension is not also present, although it is easy enough to blame the presenting symptom, e.g. asthma or epilepsy, for causing the tension. Billig in 1953 aptly described the tension as "the world looks like a sour apple", "crabbiness" and "a fall in energy".[2] Tension may be so acute and disabling that in France it is recognised for legal purposes as temporary insanity. On the other hand, in its mildest form, it may be no more than the natural contrariness of woman.

Mood Swings

The most characteristic symptom is the sudden mood swing. A woman may be conversing genially when suddenly, for no obvious reason, she becomes uncontrollably argumentative and aggressive and is indeed a "changed personality".

A 35-years-old teacher married to a headmaster stated: "For seven days during the premenstruum I became tense, shouting, irritable, weepy, tired, bloated with swelling of legs and ankles and with headaches over the eyes. I have had two children and at those times when I am in an uncontrollable temper I have hit them really hard."

She was successfully treated with progesterone for twelve months and has been free from symptoms ever since. She later wrote:

"It has been a valuable experience – I would never have believed that an intelligent woman like me, with high morals and good education, could ever lose control of herself to such an extent that she would batter her children, for I love my children dearly. How utterly illogical it is that I personally should cause them permanent damage."

The suddenness of this change of personality is something men rarely experience. However, at a recent medical meeting, a doctor with diabetes, stabilised on insulin, discussed his disease. To him the most distressing part was his inability to control his own emotions when the aggressive and quarrelsome outbursts occurred so unexpectedly as he suddenly became hypoglycaemic. There are many women with the premenstrual syndrome who would sympathise with him in his inability to be master of his own emotions. So often they find a sudden rage within them which changes them from a placid personality into an irritable, aggressive, irrational, nagging female.

Depression

Depression is manifested by weeping and a pessimistic outlook, easily relieved by congenial company. Although it is quite severe, the duration is seldom more than a few days, fourteen at the most. She feels inferior, knows that nobody cares or loves her, is unable to make decisions and is upset by the least thing, making mountains out of molehills. One woman wrote, "I want to back into a corner and stay there undisturbed like a mouse". Another woman wrote:

> "My problem is, about ten days before my period comes, I get uncontrollable fits of depression which makes me hit rock bottom. If I am with a crowd of friends I feel like I am going to suffocate, it is a feeling which comes over me and I want to run out. The same thing seems to happen to me if I am with one person. All I want to do is cry and my mind thinks of all morbid things possible. Also a very strong feeling of loneliness comes over me which makes me feel I am choking with fear. I am usually a normal woman of 28 years who has plenty of friends who I get on with very well and in general people seem to like me. But as I said before, about a week and a half before the period comes my whole personality seems to change and I feel that I can't go on much longer like this, it drains all energy from me."

Those close to the sufferer are likely to recognise her moods, and the husband will know this is not an opportune moment to discuss the family budget, and the office staff will avoid making plans, suggesting alterations or asking favours.

Another woman described the change as like "from Dr. Jekyll to Mr. Hyde. I become subject to depression, feel emotionally unstable, hysterical and miserable. Sometimes I get so keyed up that I can't sleep for 2 to 3 days before a period starts. I feel pressure across the base of my skull as if my brain was swollen."

Tears are always near the surface during the premenstruum in many women, as noted by McCance et al.[3] Their findings are shown in Fig. 4.1.

One woman gave up driving on certain days as she tended to burst into tears each time the traffic lights were against her. Another recalled "sitting

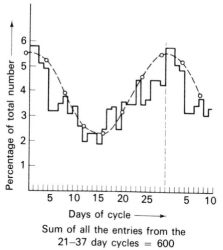

Fig. 4.1   Variation in tendency to cry throughout the menstrual cycle. (From McCance, R. A., Luff, M. C, and Widdowson, E. E. (1938), *J. Hyg.*, London, **37**, 571–611.)

in the theatre with tears rolling down my cheeks – squeezing my hands and saying to myself 'NO – I mustn't, this is a comedy – everyone else is laughing'."

The depression is especially marked in teenagers and menopausal women, and in both these groups, if charts are kept they may well reveal monthly mood swings at times of missed menstruation, as well as at menstruation. One may suspect an underlying depression if the sufferer blames some minor ailment, such as a boil, for the lethargy and malaise, creating the impression that if only this one small spot would disappear all the mental tension would go.

SUICIDES

Surveys in Britain and throughout the world into the incidence of suicides both successful and attempted, have shown that there is an increased incidence during the paramenstruum. The following case history provides a typical example:

Case 1

30-year-old housewife

Her premenstrual syndrome was recognised when she was a teenager and it became worse after marriage. During the seven premenstrual days she was irritable and tense, more aggressive and violent (often self-directed as well as directed towards husband and elder child). During the pre-menstruum she "over-reacted" to stress and became more emotional. On the first day of menstruation all symptoms eased and she became calm, friendly and rational. She was unable to tolerate the Pill, which caused depression. During her pregnancies she became free from mood swings and "happy" but had puerperal depression.

She had made five suicidal gestures each one on the last premenstrual day with an overdose of aspirins; an overdose of Valium; slashing her wrist; self-stabbing; and jumping under a train. On March 16th she lost her temper and hit her elder daughter aged five years who would not stop crying. She was then shocked by her action and asked for her children to be taken into care.

Menstruation started on the 18th March.

While it is possible that some suicides may be attributed solely to the premenstrual syndrome, it seems that in most cases there is an underlying endogenous depression in which the additional burden of premenstrual depression acts as a trigger to increase the severity until breaking point is reached. Suicidal attempts due solely to the premenstrual syndrome are characteristically preceded by a quarrel and are not premeditated; with the onset of menstruation these patients rapidly recover from their depression. Witnesses will confirm that the woman was her usual gay, vivacious self until an hour or two before the attempt. The quarrel is usually about something very unimportant – a typical storm in a teacup.

IRRITABILITY

Irritability takes an irrational form and is usually accompanied with little insight. Patients will describe themselves as "agitated – jittery – intolerant – impatient – spiteful – faultfinding – vindictive – irrational – snappy – screaming – shouting – nagging – useless – bitchy – the least thing upsets me – the children won't behave – frightening to the children – I try not to shout at the children – quarrelsome – quicktempered – I can't suffer fools gladly". Often the incident which provokes the anger has been present for some time, but suddenly the woman explodes with anger over some triviality like a coat lying on the floor, or a missing button on her husband's jacket (Fig. 4.2).

The sudden fiery outburst of irritability may be similar to the psychomotor attacks of epilepsy, and could be lightly dismissed as

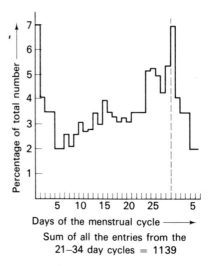

Fig. 4.2   Variation in the incidence of irritability throughout the menstrual cycle. (From McCance, R. A., Luff, M. C., and Widdowson, E. E. (1938), *J. Hyg.*, London, **37**, 571–611.)

hysteria. Irritable outbursts are likely to occur when the woman has not eaten for some considerable time and may result from transient hypoglycaemia.

During an outburst of irritability the woman may become violent and is prone to hit out at anyone within reach, often the nearest and dearest. She is generally completely unaware of the seriousness of her actions and is quite unable to prevent them. It is in this situation that the husband and/or children, can and do, get battered. The following case history is all too common:

Case 2

31-year-old secretary

The premenstrual syndrome started after second childbirth. During the seven premenstrual days she became increasingly depressed and tense, and by the third premenstrual day became very irritable, so that she might hit out at her daughters aged four and one year, if they failed to obey her command instantly. She would wake up later to find herself crying and would then realise what harm she had done. She would become so exhausted that she would spend whole days in bed. The irritability eased with the onset of menstruation, and the depression and exhaustion slowly disappeared during the six days of menstruation.

She was calm and energetic from Day 6 to 16 of each cycle. She had two court appearances for assault on her children. She flew from Milan monthly for consultations and became free from premenstrual symptoms on progesterone.

Considering the number of mothers referred for treatment of the premenstrual syndrome, who are known to have battered their own children, the overall incidence of premenstrual battering must be very high. However, there have been no surveys into this aspect of non-accidental injuries.

Often the husband describes how he knows he will be unable to do anything right and that his wife will lose her usual understanding and become a "nagger" or "bitch" for a few days. It is also at this time that the employee will suddenly leave her job after a disagreement. The Industrial Tribunal has ruled that it is unfair to dismiss a female employee who has a premenstrual tantrum. Most marriage guidance counsellors are aware of the ill consequence that can arise from premenstrual irritability and will draw the attention of both members of the marriage partnership to the relationship of quarrelling to the menstrual cycle. The wise counsellor, when telephoned urgently at the time of a marital quarrel, will arrange a meeting for seven days later when the woman is likely to be in her calm postmenstrual phase.

The irritability may ease quite suddenly. It may be replaced by a sense of guilt at the trouble the tantrums have caused. As one woman said, "I wish others would realise it wasn't the true me who caused all this".

LETHARGY

Lethargy is both mental and physical, varying from a mild physiological tiredness to an overpowering desire to sleep and the woman may even feel "too lazy to talk". It is a lethargy that is difficult to overcome, resulting in slower piece time work in the factory, impaired efficiency in the office and difficulty in composing letters, while teachers find themselves slower at marking homework and less able to maintain discipline. One teacher admitted "every month there are one or two days when I am simply not worth the salary my employers pay me". More than one secretary has been referred by her employer who noticed those few days each month when typing errors got out of control and the waste paper basket was filled to overflowing. There is a desire to perform the minimum of work and an inability to cope with even routine jobs. Creative workers may notice a lack of inspiration and should postpone more important assignments until the lethargy has passed. Manual dexterity is lost and the resultant clumsiness may lead to unnecessary breakages. Paramenstrual lethargy must be widespread in the population or it would not appear so markedly in studies of mental ability and work performance (Chapter 17).

In its more severe form it is seen in the woman who seeks refuge on the park bench on her way to work and sleeps there, or the housewife who sneaks up to bed once the family are off to work and to school. A 16-year-old girl at a boarding school was referred after the Matron had found her sleeping at her desk while other girls were out playing.

ALCOHOL EXCESS

Alcohol appears to be more intoxicating during the paramenstruum when there is water retention present. This, together with a premenstrual lack of self-control and depression, causes many women to have a monthly drinking bout, often in secret. During an investigation in a prison, several women were noted to have a record of imprisonment at monthly intervals for being drunk and disorderly. One prisoner described how she always seemed to start menstruation in the police cell shortly after her arrest. The lack of self-control at this time of the menstrual cycle is seen in the following statements:

> "I can understand all the dangers, and can control myself for about three weeks, and then it gets the better of me and I don't want to help myself any more."

> "I only take alcohol when I'm depressed, but I hate myself for doing it."

In an American survey 67% of menstruating female alcoholics related their drinking bouts to their menstrual cycle and 100% indicated that drinking had begun or increased in the premenstruum.[1]

PHOBIAS

The first acute phobic attack often occurs during a hypoglycaemic episode in the paramenstruum, but how the phobias continue after that depend more on the handling of the initial attack than on the time relationship to the menstrual cycle. When the patient is receiving behaviour therapy consideration should be given to the phase of the cycle.

DISTURBANCES OF SLEEP

Sleep disturbances are common, either hypersomnia where the woman has the greatest difficulty in getting up in the morning even after 12 hours sleep, or as insomnia with the sleep being disturbed by dreams and nightmares.

References
1. Belfer, M. L., and Carroll, M. (1971), *Arch. Gen. Psychiat.*, **25**, 540.
2. Billig, H. E. (1953), *Internat. Rec. Med.*, **11**, 166, 487.
3. McCance, R. A., Luff, M. C., and Widdowson (1937), *J. Hyg. (London)*, **37**, 571–611.

CHAPTER FIVE

Somatic Symptoms and Signs

Every system and probably every tissue in the body is affected by changes in the menstrual hormone levels. The symptoms and signs of the premenstrual syndrome, which recur at the same phase of each menstrual cycle, are not specific, and they may all occur in other women unrelated to menstruation and also may occur in men.

NEUROLOGICAL SYSTEM

Headaches

Most surveys show that after tension, headache is the next commonest symptom of the premenstrual syndrome. However, the characteristics of the headache are variable, ranging from the dull, continuous, generalised headache, easily relieved by a simple analgesic, to prostration from a classical migraine with visual and other aura, vertigo and vomiting. The site of the headache is variable, including hemicranial, bifrontal, bitemporal, occipital, vertical, over the eyes, behind the eyes or affecting one or both eyes. The time relationship of 512 headaches in sufferers of the premenstrual syndrome is shown in Fig. 5.1.

There are many mechanisms responsible for the production of headaches. Amongst those occurring predominantly during the para-menstruum the important aetiological factors are depression, water retention and hypoglycaemia. It is probable that not all menstrual migraines are hormonal in origin, and that a genetic and dietary factor may be present.

The use of the oestrogen-progestogen oral contraceptive pill increases both the frequency and the number of headaches occurring in the week without the Pill. In a nation wide study of 886 non-pregnant migraine sufferers, aged between 20–45 years and covering a total of 936 migraine attacks, a marked relationship to menstruation was shown, particularly among the pill takers (Fig. 5.2).

The patient often hesitates to record the symptoms of lethargy,

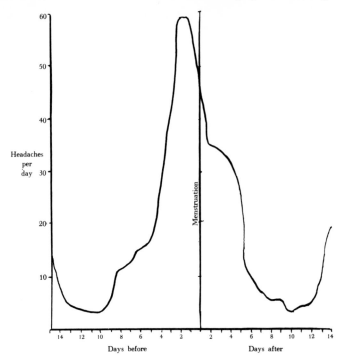

Fig. 5.1 Time relationship of 512 headaches in sufferers of the premenstrual headache. (From Dalton, K. (1973), *Headache*, **12**, 4, 151.)

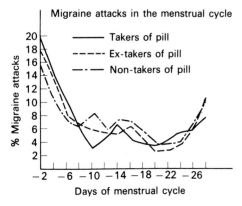

Fig. 5.2 Migraine attacks (935) in relation to the menstrual cycle. (From Dalton, K. (1976), *Headache*, **15**, 4, 247.)

irritability and depression, either because the onset is so imperceptible or because she feels that the symptoms are evidence of her lack of self-control. Headaches are therefore useful to record on a chart when investigating the relationship of symptoms to menstruation. The use of attack forms (page 15) are especially helpful in determining whether an individual attack of headache was provoked by hypoglycaemia or was due to a specific food factor, e.g. cheese, chocolate or alcohol.

Epilepsy

Epilepsy is a culminating symptom of the premenstrual syndrome, either as grand mal, which is the commoner premenstrual symptom, or petit mal. The onset may coincide with the menarche or following a pregnancy complicated by pre-eclampsia, or puerperal depression. In a survey of 192 women, who had previously suffered from pre-eclampsia, it was noted that 10 women (5%) subsequently developed premenstrual grand mal. This is a complication of pre-eclampsia which is too often overlooked. It is interesting that sufferers of premenstrual epilepsy frequently experience a severe headache prior to an attack, similar to that experienced before an eclamptic fit. These patients can be controlled by progesterone therapy, without the use of anti-convulsive drugs. Progesterone is not classified as an anti-convulsant, and so women suffering from premenstrual epilepsy controlled by progesterone, are able to apply for a driving licence when they have been free from fits for three years. It also eliminates the dangers of short- and long-term side effects of anti-convulsants.

The charts of two women whose grand mal attacks were related to menstruation are shown in Fig. 5.3. In both cases there were also premenstrual symptoms of tension and headache and attacks were precipitated by long intervals without food. Both obtained a driving licence after three years of progesterone treatment and were able to stop anti-convulsants. The mother of two children had a short relapse five years later when she developed a large progesterone abscess in her buttocks and progesterone treatment was temporarily suspended.

Vertigo

Vertigo occurs in about a third of all sufferers, either accompanying a headache or occurring alone, and is aggravated by stooping. It is common in parous women approaching the menopause, and in those who have suffered from pre-eclampsia. It is probably due to increased fluid in the labyrinths.

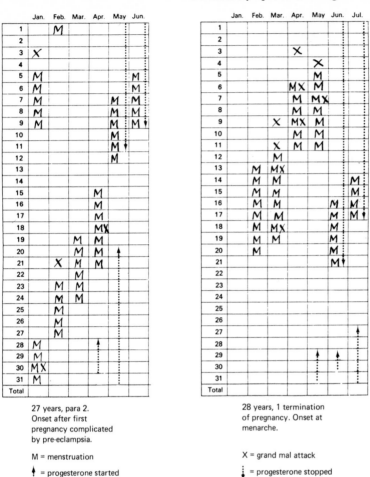

Fig. 5.3 Charts of two patients with Premenstrual Epilepsy.

Syncope

Syncope is liable to occur after prolonged standing, such as queuing for lunch. There is usually a history of a long interval without food, probably having missed breakfast.

Paraesthesia

Paraesthesia of the hands and feet is common among those with water retention and symptoms of weight gain and bloatedness. Initially the symptoms are limited to the paramenstruum, but they may increase until they are present throughout the entire month, typical of the carpal tunnel syndrome; in such cases relief may be obtained by decompression of the median nerve. Paraesthesia is noted among those whose pregnancy has been complicated with pre-eclampsia or weight gain. Occasionally the paraesthesia may represent the aura of a classical migraine attack.

SYMPTOMS OF THE RESPIRATORY SYSTEM

Asthma

Asthma often commences acutely in the middle of the night, continues for hours or days and then ends abruptly with the onset of menstruation. About a third of women of childbearing years attending asthma allergy clinics are noted to have a tendency to premenstrual attacks, especially around puberty and the menopause. The asthma is accompanied by tension, which is easily blamed onto the distress caused by the asthma attack. When recording on a chart it is worth while noting the number of occasions that an aerosol inhaler is used for the relief of symptoms.

Pneumothorax

There is an interesting report of a 41-year-old woman who had 25 recurrent attacks of right sided spontaneous pneumothorax over a period of 4 years, always on the fourth day of menstruation. At thoracotomy endometriosis of the diaphragm was found.[1]

OTO-RHINO-LARYNGOLOGICAL SYMPTOMS

Engorgement of the nasal mucous membrane occurring at menstruation is reputed to have been known by Hippocrates. It may result in nasal obstruction causing *sinusitis* or be misdiagnosed as a common cold. Recurrent colds in women of childbearing years should be regarded with suspicion and the time relationship of the attacks plotted against her menstruation. The woman who complains in April that she's already had four colds since Christmas is always suspect.

Rhinitis

Rhinitis is another common cyclical allergic phenomenon, often referred to by laymen as the 'common cold'.

Hoarseness

Hoarseness of the voice may occur during the premenstruum, but it is especially noticed in opera singers. One opera singer arranged her engagements so that they avoided the paramenstruum. Another, who was treated with progesterone for the relief of premenstrual epilepsy, remarked that the quality of her voice, and her ability to reach high notes had improved since starting treatment. The symptoms appear to be due to oedema of the vocal cords.

Diminution of the Sense of Smell

The loss of a sense of smell is probably commoner than expected. The manufacturers of a deodorant/anti-perspirant noticed that women changed their brand after three or four weeks' use, complaining that it had ceased to function effectively. It was then realised that the woman's dissatisfaction was due to a premenstrual increase in sweating and vaginal discharge and a diminishing perception of the reassuring perfume of the deodorant-anti-perspirant product. This had led women falsely to conclude that the product had lost its efficiency.

GASTRO-INTESTINAL SYMPTOMS

Abdominal bloatedness causes considerable embarrassment to those of slim build, who have to change into loose-fitting clothes. An increase in girth by 5 to 10 cm may be tolerated without complaint by the obese, but not by the figure conscious. It is best measured at the level of the umbilicus. It should be measured when lying down and when standing at different phases of the cycle. The standing measurement increases premenstrually. If there is no apparent difference in relation to menstruation it is more likely to be due to laxity of the anterior abdominal wall. Some women complain of heaviness and dragging pains associated with the bloatedness, which is a symptom of water retention.

Food Cravings and Compulsive Eating during the premenstruum are frequently noticed, and are due to alteration in glucose tolerance. It is especially noted by those on strict weight restriction diets, who can maintain their permitted food intake until the premenstruum when, coupled with lack of self-control, they gorge chocolates, sweets and high carbohydrate foods in large quantities. A slim typist described how she crept downstairs after midnight to eat two whole loaves of bread when previously she had limited herself to one slice daily. Smith and Sauder[2] noted in a questionnaire survey of 300 nurses that food cravings were positively related to premenstrual depression and water retention.

Nausea and Vomiting may occur as accompanying symptoms of headaches or bloatedness, but they rarely occur alone.

Constipation is a common premenstrual symptom related to water retention. By contrast, diarrhoea is an uncommon symptom and if a woman claims a relationship to menstruation it is important to investigate thoroughly and arrange for careful charting. On more than one occasion intermittent diarrhoea has been found to be due to Sonne dysentery.

Haemorrhoids may prove troublesome during the premenstruum and are related to constipation and water retention which occurs at this time.

Mittelschmerz, or mild cramping pain in the iliac fossa occurring at ovulation is due to the rupture of a Graafian follicle; it is included because the cyclical recurrence occurs in the same phase of each menstrual cycle, and because it rarely occurs without some mild premenstrual tension later in the cycle. The pain lasts only a few hours and may be accompanied by vaginal discharge or slight bleeding. There is no abdominal guarding, distention or vomiting, which differentiates it from other acute abdominal emergencies. It is a common cause of abdominal pain in girls from 12 to 20 years. It is important that the cause is carefully explained to the girls, as by worrying they may present repeatedly for reassurance that it is not appendicitis. Getting them to record the time of their abdominal symptoms and of menstruation, helps them to appreciate the relationship.

URINARY SYMPTOMS

Oliguria is accompanied by oedema and weight gain during the premenstruum and followed by a spontaneous diuresis during menstruation. It may be accompanied by nocturnal frequency as increased urinary excretion occurs in relation to the horizontal posture. Oliguria benefits from diuretics.

Urethritis and cystitis commonly recur during the premenstruum and may be due to the increase in vaginal discharge or to retention cysts in the urethra. In the absence of infection, progesterone treatment is most effective.

Enuresis is a troublesome symptom in an adult, but when limited to the premenstruum is amenable to treatment. It occurs in those who were late in developing bladder control in childhood and may be accompanied by hypersomnia.

Urinary retention is rarely seen during the paramenstruum, and appears to result from oedema of the urinary sphincter. A 17-year-old boarding school girl was admitted to hospital on eight occasions for premenstrual urinary retention. Full renal investigations were normal, and then it was noted that the dates of hospital admissions were correlated with the dates of menstruation. She was successfully treated with progesterone.

SYMPTOMS OF THE MUSCULO-SKELETAL SYSTEM

Joint and muscle pains may be noted only during the premenstruum especially when there is a history of injury, and characteristically there is increased pain and stiffness on waking. Pains may be present for a few days in the back, hip, knees, ankles, shoulders, hands and feet and then miraculously vanish only to reappear with the next premenstruum. The pain can be due to localised oedema, or to failure of muscle relaxation. The most likely candidates are parous women over 35 years.

BREAST SYMPTOMS

Breast enlargement with pain and tenderness of the nipples tends to start at ovulation, and increases in severity until the onset of menstruation. Transient masses or cysts may occur in the breast premenstrually, these disappear spontaneously or decrease in size during menstruation. It is akin to the breast activity which occurs early in pregnancy.

CARDIO-VASCULAR SYMPTOMS

Palpitations, Ectopic Beats and Paroxysmal Tachycardia have all been reported during the premenstruum. All call for a full cardiological investigation as well as the recording of symptoms in relation to menstruation. There may be accompanying dyspnoea, weight gain and oedema.

Varicose veins may only become visible during the premenstruum or may only become painful with a bursting sensation at this time. It is suggested that the pain is due to increased tissue fluid stretching the fascia with venous distention and decreased venous tone.

DERMATOLOGICAL SYMPTOMS

Boils, Acne and Herpes are the most common premenstrual symptoms. Skin disorders have a cyclical variation in relation to menstruation, either recurrent with intervals of normality or exacerbations of previously existing skin lesions.

Facial pigmentation waxes and wanes with each menstruation due to increasing secretion of melanocyte stimulating hormone of the pituitary. **Urticaria** may recur as an allergic reaction but the allergen is unknown.

EYE SYMPTOMS

Conjunctivitis of the non-infective type may occur either unilaterally or bilaterally, and presents as a red, watery irritable eye. Its relationship to the menstrual cycle was noted as early as the sixteenth century. It may be accompanied by sneezing, and may be related to the premenstrual engorgement of the nasal mucuos membrane causing reflex stimulation of the fifth cranial nerve.

Styes are another common recurrent symptom related to the lowered resistance to infection during the paramenstruum.

Glaucoma

Premenstrual syndrome and closed angle glaucoma have many points of similarity thus: (1) can be provoked by the water drinking test, (2) are more severe in the early morning, (3) are increased or precipitated by stress and fatigue, (4) are accompanied by other systemic disturbances such as nausea, lethargy and vertigo. In a survey at the Institute of Ophthalmology, London, 89% of sufferers of closed angle glaucoma also had premenstrual syndrome, compared with only 50% among those with simple chronic glaucoma.[1] Again there was a high incidence 21% of pre-eclampsia among the parous sufferers of all types of glaucoma. The timing of 356 episodes of ocular symptoms in 106 menstrual cycles showed 49% occurred during the paramenstruum. The influence of menstruation on the timing of ocular symptoms was almost entirely confined to the closed-angle glaucoma with 60% occurring during the paramenstruum (Fig. 5.4) compared with 30% among those with simple chronic glaucoma (Fig. 5.5).

Regular observations have shown a pattern of raised intra-ocular pressure with a simultaneous rise in blood pressure and weight during the paramenstruum. Each patient has her own timing of the rise, some show a rise in the premenstruum, followed by a drop during menstruation before returning to the intermenstrual level, and other women show a premenstrual drop followed by a marked menstrual rise before returning to normality (Fig. 5.6).

Contact lenses become a problem among sufferers of the premenstrual syndrome, who should be advised to have all the fittings, and to first start wearing them, during the postmenstruum. One frequently hears the

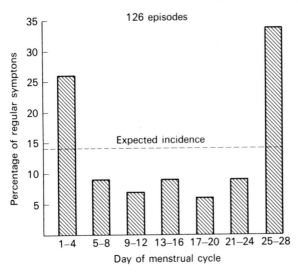

Fig. 5.4 Ocular symptoms in closed angle glaucoma in relation to the menstrual cycle. (From *Brit. J. Ophthal.* (1967), 51, 10, 692.)

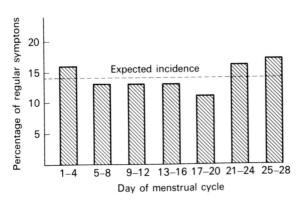

Fig. 5.5 Ocular symptoms in simple chronic glaucoma in relation to the menstrual cycle. (From *Brit. J. Opthal.* (1967), 51, 10, 692.)

remark after progesterone treatment, "Now I can wear my contact lenses all the month round."

Conjunctival and Retinal Haemorrhages may result from premenstrual capillary fragility.

Behcet's Syndrome with its triad of relapsing iridocyclitis and

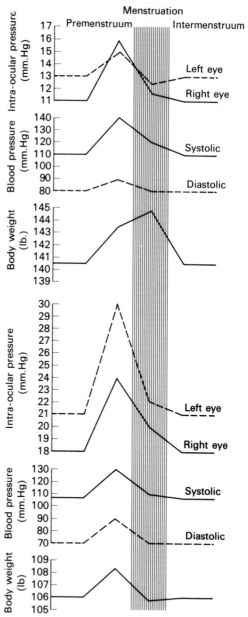

Fig. 5.6   Intra-ocular pressure, blood pressure and weight in patients with closed angle glaucoma. (From *Brit. J. Ophthal.* (1967), 51, 10, 692.)

associated recurrent ulceration of the mouth and genitalia has been noted to have a periodicity coincident with menstruation.

Uveitis tends to have recurrences during the paramenstruum.

Dental Symptoms

Ulcerative Stomatitis and Buccal Ulceration occurring during the premenstruum can be independent or may occur coincidently with ulceration of the vulva, lower vagina or anus. In some cases it may be due to recurrent herpes.

Drug Reactions

These are common during the premenstruum and may follow administration of antibiotics and inoculations. Confusion may occur as to the real origin of such reactions. In double blind clinical trials the placebo drugs are often reported to have side effects such as increased drowsiness, headache, nausea, or increased pain, which may be no more than the usual premenstrual symptoms which have been meticulously observed and reported.

Cosmetic Symptoms

During the premenstruum the woman may be conscious of not looking her best due to a puffy face, thick lips, dark shadows under her eyes, the presence of acne and pimples, and lank, greasy hair.

SIGNS

Oedema

Oedema of the ankles (especially in those whose work involved prolonged standing), abdomen and fingers are common, but does not occur in all patients. It may be noticed by the patient when her shoes will not tie up, her wedding ring becomes too tight, her dresses no longer fit comfortably, she develops facial pallor, or her dentures no longer fit due to swelling of the gums. Characteristically, oedema increases in the hot weather. When oedema is already present, as in congenital lymphatic oedema or lymphatic obstruction following radical mastectomy, there may be a further increase during the premenstruum.

Fluctuations of blood pressure throughout the menstrual cycle are frequent, with rises of 20 to 30 mm during the premenstruum or preceding the onset of symptoms. Rises from 110/70 to 140/90 may occur, but rarely does it rise to hypertensive levels. On the other hand, hypotension may occur when the onset of an attack is sudden and accompanied by marked oedema. A severe case of premenstrual cyclical oedema has been described in which a 34-year-old woman sometimes gained as much as 5 kg in less than 24 hours, and these episodes were accompanied by severe shock and hypotension.

Albuminuria may occasionally occur in severe cases during the premenstruum, especially in those prone to epilepsy. For its detection it is necessary to use either catheter specimens or carefully collected midstream specimens, as slight menstrual staining may otherwise contaminate the urine. One patient was diagnosed as having "orthostatic albuminuria", but later it was noted that the albuminuria only occurred premenstrually at times of severe symptoms.

Fig. 5.7 shows observations on a 40-year-old housewife with no children, who was suffering from premenstrual headaches, depression and

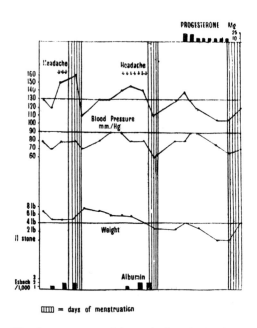

Fig. 5.7   Blood pressure, weight and albumin in the premenstrual syndrome.

irritability. There was a rise in blood pressure from 110/70 mm after menstruation to 140–160/80 mm Hg in the premenstruum, and the albuminuria in catheter specimens was limited to the premenstruum. Treatment with progesterone brought relief of all symptoms, the blood pressure did not rise and there was no albuminuria.

Fig. 5.8 shows observations on a 42-year-old housewife with no children, who was suffering from premenstrual headache, depression, oedema and dyspnoea. It shows a weight gain of 5 kg in a 44·5 kg woman, this weight being lost by diuresis during menstruation. Albuminuria was

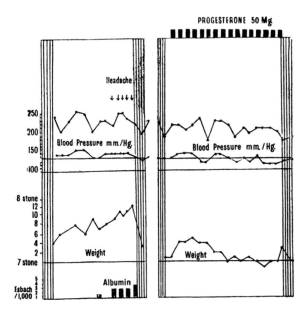

Fig. 5.8   Blood pressure, weight and albumin in the premenstrual syndrome with essential hypertension.

present in the premenstruum and early morning measurements of the ankle circumference showed an increase from 18·4 cm to 24·6 cm. At the height of the oedema moist sounds were present in the bases of both lungs, accounting no doubt for the dyspnoea. The blood pressure was raised throughout the cycle at a level of 200–250/120–130 mm Hg. On treatment with progesterone she became symptom-free, her weight and ankle circumference remained steady, and there was no albuminuria. Nevertheless, the raised blood pressure persisted at its previous high level throughout the cycle.

Fig. 5.9 shows observations on a 40-year-old club hostess, who had been unemployed for six months owing to premenstrual epileptic fits and migraine. She was a widow, whose only pregnancy had been terminated at 28 weeks because of chronic nephritis. Immediately prior to an epileptic fit she had a blood pressure of 190/110 mm Hg, which dropped to

120–130/80 mm Hg after menstruation. Premenstrually her weight rose by 0·9 kg and the ankle circumference increased from 19 cm to 22 cm. The albuminuria was present throughout the cycle. When treated with progesterone she became symptom free, blood pressure, weight and ankle

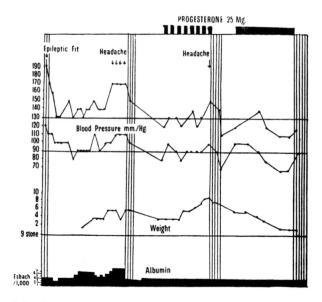

Fig. 5.9 Blood pressure, weight and albumin in the premenstrual syndrome with chronic nephritis.

circumference becoming steady, but the albuminuria persisted throughout the cycle. No epileptic fits have occurred since commencing progesterone 20 years ago.

Spontaneous bruising may occur due to increased capillary fragility during the premenstruum. The bruises are painless, bilateral, usually all about the same size and circular. Common sites are the thighs and upper arms. One such spontaneous bruise was observed developing on the upper arm while at rest and spread from a sudden red dot to a bruise which reached a diameter of 2·6 cm. It was quite painless and the time from first noticing it to its completion took barely a minute. Hess's test (with 80 mm Hg for 10 minutes) may be used to test capillary fragility in women and an increase during premenstruum, rising to a maximum around the first day of menstruation, may be noted. There are considerable individual variations in maximal fragilities, European women tend to have higher fragilities than Chinese or Malaysian women.

References

1. Kirschner, P. A., Delaleu, S., and Prusansky, M. (1973), **73**, 2693.
2. Smith, S. L. and Sauder, C. (1969), *Psychosom. Med.*, **31**, 4, 281.

CHAPTER SIX

Incidence

The premenstrual syndrome has been described as "one of the world's commonest diseases", but the true incidence is difficult to assess. The diagnosis of the premenstrual syndrome with the many, varied somatic and psychological symptoms depends partly on the intelligence of the patient and partly on her medical adviser. It is likely that as members of the public become increasingly more educated by the media on menstrual problems the incidence of the premenstrual syndrome may appear to increase.

Another aspect of the problem is that in some of the surveys, women suffering from recognised somatic symptoms have been deliberately excluded as when "all those on regular medication or suffering from organic disease" are not included in the population studied. Other surveys are carried out in factories which do not employ epileptics, or among university students with above average intelligence. In yet other surveys, usually by psychologists, a menstrual distress questionnaire is used, emphasising the psychological symptoms. The incidence of the premenstrual syndrome depends on the criteria adopted. Thus Pennington[5] found an incidence of 95% whilst Logan and Cushion[4] found it to be 6·5% in their general practice. Neither of these figures is likely to be correct. Kessel and Coppen[3] in a survey into the menstrual problems of 500 English women, chosen at random from ten practitioners' lists, concluded that the incidence was very high, and that there were two very common but distinct entities – the premenstrual syndrome and dysmenorrhoea.

In 1954, a survey of 825 women in north London used the definition: "Those whose premenstrual symptoms have been present for three menstrual cycles as confirmed by a prospective calendar, and with symptoms severe enough to demand medical attention or loss of work in the past three months." The incidence was found to be 27% for controls and 86% among women who had previously suffered from pre-eclampsia. If one uses less strict criteria, to include symptoms endured or self-treated, and not confirming the relationship to menstruation with a calendar, an incidence of 40% may be expected in Britain.

There is a need for more surveys to be carried out in speciality clinics, e.g. asthma, obesity, epilepsy, cardiac, infertility, colitis, hypertension or otitis clinics, to determine the proportion of women who have exacerbations of their distress at the time of menstruation, and those whose symptoms are only present in the paramenstruum.

AGE AND PARITY

The age and parity of 100 consecutive patients referred to the premenstrual syndrome clinic at University College Hospital, London, by their general practitioners because of severe premenstrual syndrome, which had not responded to the treatment, are shown in Table 6.1.

Table 6.1

Age and Parity of 100 Consecutive Hospital Patients with the Premenstrual Syndrome

Age of 100 patients		Parity of 100 patients	
Under 20 years	0	No pregnancies	19
21–30 years	19	Abortion only	6
31–40 years	44	1 child	21
41–50 years	34	2 children	27
Over 50 years	3	3 children	17
		4 or more children	10

The premenstrual syndrome is usually not a problem in women under 20 years of age, but becomes more troublesome after the age of 30. Lloyd emphasised the fact that hitherto unaffected women often begin to experience the premenstrual syndrome in their fourth decade and suggested the designation "mid-thirties syndrome" although this is not to imply that the condition differs substantially from that involving women in other groups. On the other hand, it is present in the younger age group, for instance, it was noted that among 78 patients admitted with acute psychiatric illnesses during menstruation, 37% were under 25 years, compared with 20% for those over 45 years (Fig. 6.1).

Parity tends to increase with age and premenstrual symptoms increase with parity. In the previous table it can be seen that most patients were over 30 and that there was a high parity in these patients. Only 19% were nulliparous and 54% had at least two pregnancies. Not all sufferers have an easy conception, for Benedek-Jaszmann and Hearn-Sturtevant[1] studied 45 patients with the premenstrual syndrome, who were attending an infertility clinic in the Netherlands. Where coitus is avoided at times of ovulatory migraine or mittelschmerz conception is difficult.

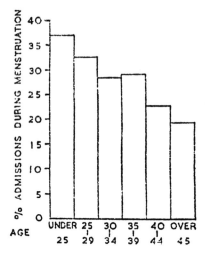

Fig. 6.1   Age distribution of 78 psychiatric patients admitted during menstruation.

PRE-ECLAMPSIA

It has already been mentioned that 86% of women who have had a pregnancy complicated by pre-eclampsia, subsequently developed pre-menstrual symptoms. Of the 100 patients in Table 6.1, 75 had full-term pregnancies and 15 (20%) suffered from pre-eclampsia. This is a similar finding to that of Greene and Dalton[2] in 1953 who reported that in 58 parous women with the premenstrual syndrome 11 (19%) gave a history of pre-eclampsia. It was this finding which led to the survey into the incidence of the premenstrual syndrome in women who had previously suffered a pre-eclamptic pregnancy and led, ultimately, to the appreciation of the diseases (Chapter 15).

There are several patients with the premenstrual syndrome under my care in whose case history there is a note that their mother had an eclamp-tic fit during the patient's birth, but the exact incidence of premenstrual syndrome among those whose mothers had eclampsia at their birth is not yet known.

PUERPERAL DEPRESSION

Among the 81 women who had been pregnant (including six abortions) in the hospital series, a total of 59 (73%) had suffered from puerperal depression. Many workers have confirmed the clinical impression that severe premenstrual syndrome may follow puerperal depression (Chapter 16).

TIME OF ONSET

The time of onset of the premenstrual syndrome is difficult to pinpoint, as it often has a gradual onset with slowly increasing severity of symptoms. It is commonly attributed to puberty, marriage, childbirth or menopause, although stress plays a part. Marriage is frequently mentioned, but this may only be because it is the husband who first recognised symptoms which may have passed unnoticed when the woman was single. Some patients were asked at each visit when their symptoms began and different answers were received on each occasion. A 34-year-old housewife attending for premenstrual migraine first mentioned symptoms of six months' duration which she attributed to domestic stress, later this period was extended to two years, dating from her second pregnancy, complicated with pre-eclampsia; on another occasion marriage at 21 years was blamed, and yet later she stated it had been present ever since her early schooldays. Undoubtedly her headaches had been present since puberty, but they only became severe at times of stress and these were the times when she sought treatment.

FAMILIAL INCIDENCE

The mother who suffers from the premenstrual syndrome may find that her daughter suffers from the same symptoms as herself and she is most likely to recognise and diagnose it in her daughter at adolescence. But the mother who suffered from spasmodic dysmenorrhoea in her youth is often surprised when her daughter develops similar symptoms after having two or three years of pain-free menstruation.

The familial incidence is high, not only for this syndrome, but also for individual symptoms. Thus several members of two or three generations have been seen who all have the same manifestation, e.g. epilepsy, depression, migraine, asthma or rhinitis. This may not be surprising as migraine and allergic phenomenon are frequently familial manifestations.

POST-HYSTERECTOMY AND POST-OOPHORECTOMY SYMPTOMS

Cyclical symptoms, of the same type as the individual's previous premenstrual symptoms, may occur after hysterectomy, bilateral oophorectomy, or artificial menopause by radiotherapy, although there is usually an interval of 6 to 12 months before the symptoms resume their full severity (Chapter 18). In one series of 34 women who had a hysterectomy for non-malignant conditions, as many as 74% had cyclically recurrent headaches. In half of these women the headaches had in fact occurred premenstrually before operative intervention, but the headaches increased in intensity after hysterectomy, often accompanied by vomiting, photophobia and blurred vision.

EFFECT OF THE ORAL CONTRACEPTIVE PILL

Contrary to the statement in pharmaceutical literature, it is my clinical experience that most patients with premenstrual syndrome cannot tolerate the Pill and readily develop side effects. In the hospital series of 100 women with severe premenstrual syndrome 56 had never taken the Pill, but of the remaining 44 women 40 (91%) developed side effects on the Pill and had changed, of their own accord, to some other method of contraception. In a recent nationwide migraine survey it was found that among previous Pill takers 81% of those with menstrual migraine had found the Pill increased the severity of the migraine.

References

1. Benedek-Jaszmann, L. J., and Hearn-Sturtevant, M. D. (1976), *Lancet,* **1,** 1095.
2. Greene, R., and Dalton, K. (1953), *Brit. med. J.,* **1,** 1007.
3. Kessel, N., and Coppen, A. (1963), *Lancet,* **2,** 61.
4. Logan, W. P. D., and Cushion (1958), *Morbidity Statistics in Gen. Pract.,* Vol. 1 (General), H.M.S.O., London.
5. Pennington, V. M. (1957), *J. Amer. med. Assn.,* **164,** 638.

CHAPTER SEVEN

Aetiology

The aetiology of the premenstrual syndrome is still incomplete, but long-held theory, accredited to Hippocrates, that "the agitated blood was seeking a channel of escape from the womb" is fast receding into the limbo of forgotten theories.

To be satisfactory any aetiology must take into account today's known and observed facts about the syndrome:

1. The cyclical relationship of the psychological and somatic symptoms to the menstrual cycle.
2. Persistence of cyclical symptoms after a hysterectomy or bilateral oophorectomy (Chapter 18).
3. The tendency of symptoms to continue, and often increase, at the time of the menopause (Chapter 18).
4. The increased intensity of symptoms at times of stress.
5. The frequent presence of sodium and water retention and potassium depletion during the premenstruum (Chapter 3).
6. The occurrence of hypoglycaemia in the premenstruum (Chapter 3).
7. The occurrence of allergic symptoms and lowered resistance to pain and infection during the premenstruum.
8. The disappearance of psychological and somatic symptoms during pregnancy in a high proportion of sufferers usually coupled with a feeling of wellbeing (Chapter 17).
9. The remarkable similarity of the premenstrual syndrome to pre-eclampsia, and the high incidence of premenstrual syndrome in those who have previously suffered from pre-eclampsia (Chapter 15).
10. The high incidence of the premenstrual syndrome after a pregnancy complicated by puerperal depression (Chapter 16).
11. The success of progesterone therapy in the relief of both psychological and somatic symptoms of the syndrome (Chapter 9).
12. The relative failure of the oral progestogens to bring the same

universal relief and the fact that the progestogens lower the blood progesterone level (Chapter 8).

It is a long journey from that theory of Hippocrates to our present-day knowledge of the hypothalamic-pituitary-ovarian axis. Frank first described premenstrual tension in 1931 and postulated that it was caused by the high level of oestrogen in the blood as a result of defective renal excretion of this hormone. He claimed that the patient's blood contained twice the normal amount of "ovarian hormone" and that after relief of symptoms by irradiation of the ovaries the level of ovarian hormones became normal.

The psychological emphasis of the words "premenstrual tension" has occupied the psychologists and psychiatrists to this day and a veritable mountain of research papers has been produced by those studying the psychological aspects of premenstrual tension, which has now become an important behavioural study for the psychologist.

In 1975 Rosseinsky and Hall[2] suggested an evolutionary theory for premenstrual tension based upon "a normal inheritance of a programmed behaviour pattern . . . having erstwhile evolutionary value". The suggestion is that in the premenstruum the female became hostile to the attentions of the male and he, in his frustration, intensified his male ardour at the next period of fertility, clearly enhancing the probability of conception. "The effect on specie survival can thus be deemed to have impressed on the hormonal/ovulation cycle, a periodic, equally programmed premenstrual tension hostility phase, of entirely normal evolutionary origin." Thus it is concluded, "premenstrual tension is intrinsic and ineradicable". But of course the authors ignore the evidence that only a portion of the female population suffer from premenstrual tension. If they were right every woman would be affected instead of the estimated 40%. In a later letter the authors state, "we were well aware of the obvious physiological effects . . . we concentrated on the tension (implying behavioural) aspect of premenstrual tension". In short they are ignoring the factual data and exploring the realms of fantasy.

Israel in 1938 found a raised renal threshold for oestrogens in fewer than half his patients, which led him to suggest that the cause was not so much the high level of oestradiol in the blood as the lack of progesterone to act as an antagonist. This concept of high oestradiol/progesterone ratio was tentatively supported by Greene and Dalton in 1953 because of their success in treating this syndrome with progesterone. They pointed out that this hypothesis does not depend on the demonstration of a consistently high level of oestradiol or a low level of progesterone, but on the ratio between the two.

Geiringer noted as early as 1951 that it is not only the ovarian hormones which fluctuate regularly throughout the normal menstrual cycle, but that those of the adrenal cortex also exhibit cyclical activity which is increased in the week preceding menstruation. With our increased knowledge of endocrinology in 1977 we should now be able to reach forward to another hypothesis.

The occurrence of the symptoms with a time relationship to menstruation suggests that a menstrual controlling centre, in the hypothalamus, is implicated in the aetiology. The hypothalamus is easily affected by cerebral stimuli. This explains why the menstrual pattern is altered at times of stress, producing an increase in the intensity and duration of premenstrual symptoms. Cyclical symptoms persist after a hysterectomy and/or oophorectomy, which suggests that the aetiological site does not lie within the uterus or ovaries, but might be in the hypothalamus, pituitary, adrenals or elsewhere.

If the symptoms were directly related to menstruation or the products of menstruation, it would be expected that symptoms would improve as the menstrual loss becomes scanty at the time of the menopause, with a complete relief of symptoms as menstruation finally ceases. However, this is not the case, for frequently there is an increase of symptoms at the time of the menopause, and cyclical symptoms may persist for some years after the cessation of menstruation. At the menopause the ovarian secretion decreases, but on the other hand, the gonadotrophins increase and the activity of adrenal cortex increases and only after some years does it decrease.

From the hypothalamus, releasing factors stimulate the pituitary gland, which as a result releases follicle stimulating hormone (FSH) and luteinising hormone (LH) to act on the ovary. The ovary secretes oestrogen in varying amounts throughout the cycle but progesterone only during the luteal phase. At each stage of this pathway there is a feed-back mechanism, the most important one, as regards our present discussion, is that which passes from the uterus to the hypothalamus and pituitary, the "progesterone feed-back pathway". It seems likely that it is this feed-back pathway which is at fault in the premenstrual syndrome.

In the anterior lobe of the pituitary, *prolactin* is secreted and this acts as a controlling mechanism on the feed-back pathways. In the hypothalamus there is a centre responsible for the secretion of a *prolactin-inhibiting factor* (PIF) which inhibits the continual release of prolactin. Hypothalamic levels of PIF appear to be depleted in cases of stress,

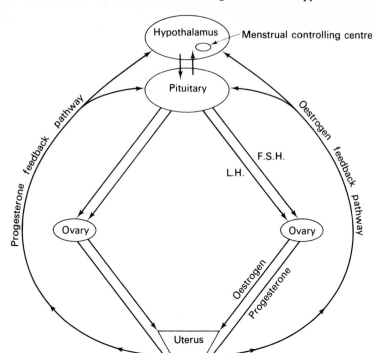

Fig. 7.1   Hormonal pathways of menstruation.

lactation, and by the administration of oestrogens, progestogens, tricyclic anti-depressants and phenothiazines (Fig. 7.2). Prolactin inhibits progesterone secretion by the luteal cells.

It would appear that in the premenstrual syndrome the fault is at the level of the progesterone feed-back pathway, either by insufficient stimulus, in which case administration of progesterone will provide the extra stimulus, or by interference due to hyperprolactinaemia, in which the prolactin may be reduced by the administration of bromocriptine, or overcome by the administration of excess progesterone.

The hypothesis of a faulty progesterone feed-back pathway would explain why progesterone levels are often low in the luteal phase, why only a proportion of sufferers have hyperprolactinaemia, why bromocriptine is not as universally successful in treatment as progesterone, and why patients with the premenstrual syndrome have difficulty in tolerating the oral contraceptive Pill, which inhibits PIF secretion.

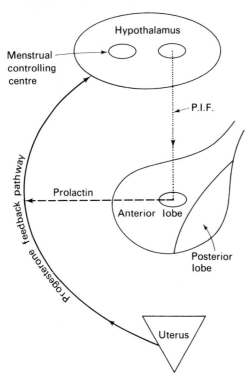

Fig. 7.2 Progesterone feed-back pathway.

The effect of the interruption in the progesterone feed-back pathway, would in turn result in diminished stimulation to the adrenal cortex, and account for disturbances of mineralocorticoids, and glucocorticoids. Progesterone is responsible for the transport of the glucocorticoids attached to the alphaglobulin in the plasma. Progesterone is one of the few steroids with a high affinity for this binding protein and can cause displacement of cortisol to the free active fraction. These glucocorticoids maintain the liver glycogen and help to maintain the blood sugar levels.[1]

References

1. Harper, H. A. (1969), *Review of Physiological Chemistry*, 12th edition. Los Altos, California: Lange Medical.
2. Munday, M. (1977), *Curr. Med. Res. Opin.* 4, Symposium Suppl. **4**, 16.
3. Rosseinsky, D. R., and Hall, P. G. (1974), *Lancet*, **2**, 1024.

CHAPTER EIGHT

The Differences between Progesterone and Progestogens

The basic steroid ring structure has played a vital part in biochemical evolution of plants and animals. Relatively small changes in the degree of unsaturation and the number and nature of substituents have a striking influence on the biochemical activity of compounds such as are shown in Fig. 8.3. It is therefore not surprising that superficially similar synthetic derivatives have different actions from natural hormones.

PROGESTERONE

The corpus luteum hormone was first isolated by Corner and Allen in 1929, and given the name "progesterone" by the Special Conference of the Health Organisation of the League of Nations in 1935.

Progesterone is secreted in the corpus luteum and passes from the ovary to the endometrium in increasing amounts from the time of ovulation. It reaches a peak of about 15 µg/ml in the plasma about Day 21 to 23 and then the level falls until the onset of menstruation. Thus the time of premenstrual symptoms coincides with the presence of progesterone in the blood (Fig. 8.1).

During pregnancy, progesterone is secreted from the ovary in increasing amounts for the first three months. The secretion of progesterone from the placenta starts about the 9th week and then is secreted in increasing amounts until the 32nd week, when it probably remains steady until term and reaches a mean of 150 µg/ml plasma (Fig. 8.2).

The functions of progesterone are to promote:

1. The proliferation of the endometrium
2. The maintenance of pregnancy
3. The development of breast tissue

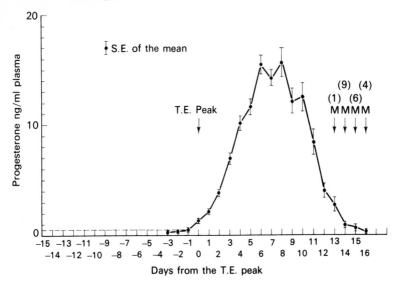

Fig. 8.1 Mean plasma progesterone levels during 20 normal menstrual cycles. (From Johansson, E. D. B. (1969), *Acta Endocrin.*, Copenhagen, **61**, 592.)

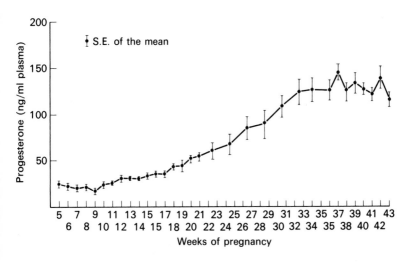

Fig. 8.2 Mean plasma progesterone levels during pregnancy. (From Johansson, E. D. B. (1969), *Acta Endocrin.*, Copenhagen, **61**, 607.)

4. The synthesis of corticosteroids in the adrenal cortex
5. The transport of glucocorticoids

The action of progesterone is species specific, for instance in man it reduces water and sodium retention, but in dogs progesterone causes water retention. It is perhaps significant to mention that no other species suffers from pre-eclampsia but the human.

Progesterone is derived from cholesterol and is essential for the synthesis of a large number of steroid hormones, including the corticosteroids, the androgens and the oestrogens (Fig. 8.3).

The major metabolite of progesterone is pregnanediol, which can be isolated quantitatively in a 24-hour urine collection. Varying proportions of the metabolites are excreted in the urine, in the bile via faeces, in the expired air and the skin.

Progesterone has a short half-life in the blood of only a few minutes. It cannot be administered by mouth as it passes via the portal system to the liver where it is rapidly metabolised; however, it can be administered by intra-muscular injections, or rectally or vaginally, or by implantation into the fat of the abdominal wall. Nillius and Johansson[4] have suggested that when given by injection progesterone is absorbed into the fat cells where it forms a depot, and diffuses back slowly into the bloodstream when the plasma level declines.

Occasionally when an intra-muscular injection of progesterone is given, the patient tastes it in her mouth within three minutes. This is due to the rapid metabolism of progesterone, the metabolite pregnanediol being excreted from the lungs.

PROGESTOGENS

Progestogens are synthetic substances which have the same action as progesterone in being able to cause endometrial withdrawal bleeding in immature oestrogen primed rabbits in the Clauberg test, they have the advantage that they can be administered by mouth or by long acting injections. On the Clauberg test some progestogens are not strongly active, while others, such as D-norgesterel, are some 2,000 times more potent than natural progesterone.

Although the formulae of progesterone, oestrogen, testosterone and cortisone are seen to be remarkably similar (Fig. 8.3) they have significantly different functions. The formulae of the various synthetic progestogens shown in Fig. 8.4 likewise resemble progesterone, testosterone and oestrogen, yet they have different properties.

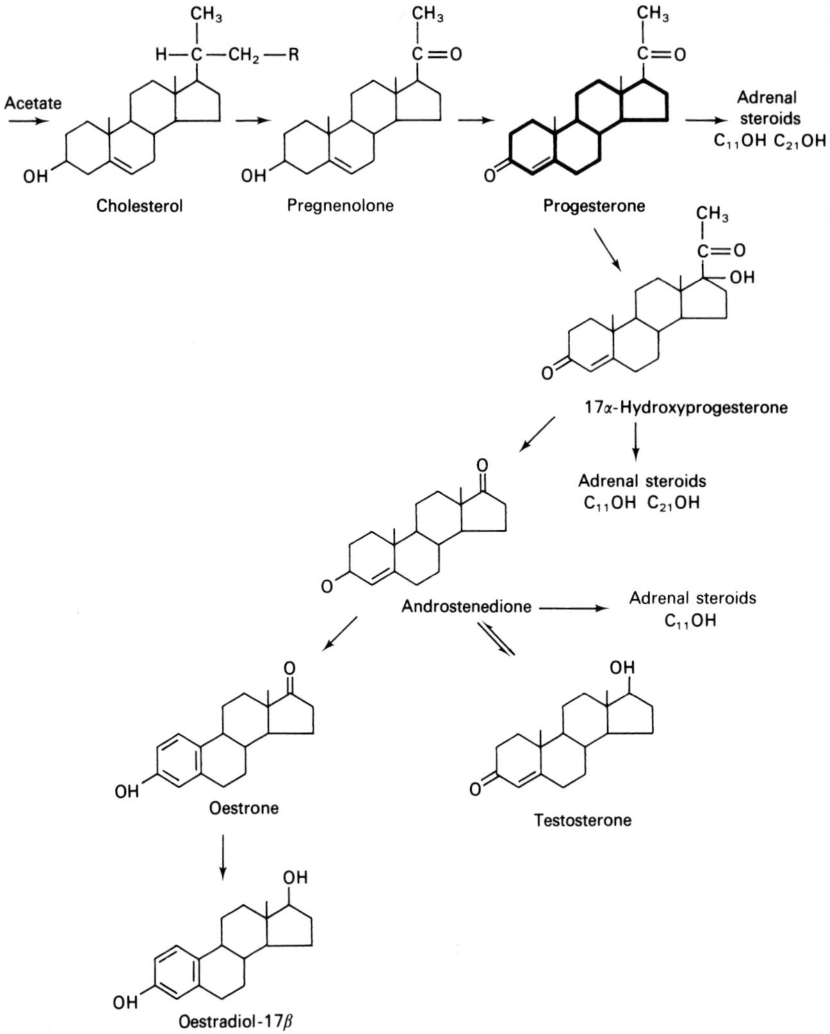

Fig. 8.3 Pathways of steroid biosynthesis in the gonads showing the key position of progesterone. (From *Hormonal Assays and their Clinical Applications* (1971), Loraine, J. A., and Bell, E. T. E. and S. Livingstone.)

It must be appreciated that the synthetic long-acting injections of 17-α-hydroxyprogesterone hexanoate and 17-α-hydroxyprogesterone caproate are not the same as the naturally occurring 17-α-hydroxyprogesterone (Figs. 8.3 and 8.4).

Before the advent of the Pill nor-ethisterone was known as nor-ethinyl

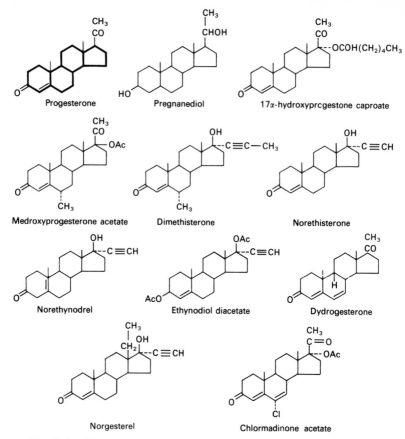

Fig. 8.4 Formulae of common progesterones. (From *Principles of Gynaecology* (1975), Jeffcote, Sir N., p. 691, Fig. 599. London: Butterworth.)

testosterone. Some of the progestogens, particularly the testosterone derivatives and 19 nor-steroids (such as ethisterone, dimethisterone, norethynodral and norethisterone) are androgenic, while others (such as dydrogesterone) are free from androgenic effects. Some progestogens (norethisterone acetate and norethynodrel) have oestrogenic activity which is absent in others (medroxyprogesterone). Progesterone is thermogenic, raising the basal body temperature, while most progestogens do not possess this action, although ethisterone is mildly thermogenic. Progesterone is not anabolic although some progestogens are.

DIFFERENCES

Whereas progesterone causes endometrial proliferation the progestogens cause accelerated glandular response leading to secretory exhaustion. This can be a useful property in gynaecological disorders, such as endometriosis and menorrhagia.

Progesterone causes a reduction in sodium and water retention while progestogens, especially norethisterone, causes an increase in sodium and water retention. Progesterone is synthesised in the adrenal cortex into corticosteroids and is used for the transport of glucocorticoids in the blood. Progestogens cannot be synthesised into the other corticosteroids in the adrenal cortex nor can they be used for the transport of glucocorticoids. Progestogens cannot, therefore, be expected to be effective in the relief of those symptoms which are due to water retention, hypoglycaemia, or in allergic reactions.

The major metabolite of progesterone is pregnanediol, but this is not found after the metabolism of progestogens.

The function of progesterone is the maintenance of pregnancy and when administered after ovulation it assists conception, especially in the cases of defective luteal phase. The most valuable contribution of the progestogens has been in the field of contraception, when administered from the fifth day of the cycle. Most (except dydrogesterone) inhibit ovulation, and increase the viscosity of the cervical mucus.

When progesterone is administered during pregnancy it has no detrimental effect on the foetus, in fact surveys have shown that it may result in enhanced intelligence and educational attainment in the child of that pregnancy (Chapter 21). In contrast when progestogens, particularly the 19 norsteroids and testosterone derivatives, have been administered during early pregnancy it has resulted in masculinisation of the female foetus.

Progesterone is not carcinogenic, in fact it has been successfully used in the treatment of stilboestrol-associated vaginal adenocarcinoma.[1] However, there are a group of progestogens which are suspected of being carcinogenic as they have been found to produce breast tumours in beagle dogs, a species prone to develop breast tumours. This has resulted in two progestogens, chlormadinone and megestrol, being withdrawn from the market.

EFFECT OF PROGESTOGENS ON THE PROGESTERONE PLASMA LEVEL

Perhaps the most important difference from the therapeutic angle is the fact that the administration of progestogens has been shown to lower the progesterone blood level.[2] Fig. 8.5 shows plasma levels of progesterone during the luteal phase of a normal cycle compared with levels in the same

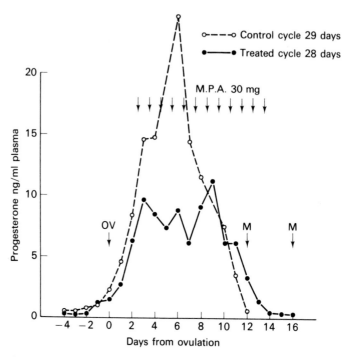

Fig. 8.5   Plasma levels of progesterone during the luteal phase of a normal cycle compared with the levels in the same women during treatment with 30 mg medroxyprogesterone acetate daily for 12 days. (From Johansson, E. D. B. (1971),*Amer. J. Obs. Gynaec.*, 110, 4, 470.)

woman during treatment with 30 mg medroxyprogesterone acetate daily for 12 days. This effect is dose dependent, with an even more pronounced lowering of progesterone plasma levels when 60 mg were administered.

Similar effects on the reduction of plasma progesterone have been demonstrated following the administration of norethisterone, d-norgesterel and chlormadinone.

The differences between progesterone and progestogens are given in

Table 8.1. Both are valuable in therapeutics but they are not inter-changeable and progestogens are not just a convenient synthetic oral substitute for progesterone, and they should have no place in the treatment of the premenstrual syndrome, or the maintenance of pregnancy.

Table 8.1

Differences between Progesterone and Progestogens

Occurrence	Progesterone Naturally occurring	Progestogen Synthetic
Route of administration	I.m. injections rectal, vaginal and implantation	Oral and long-acting injections
Clauberg test	Positive, used as standard	Potent, up to × 2,000
Effect on endometrium	Proliferation	Accelerated response followed by secre-tory exhaustion
Oestrogenic	No	Some
Androgenic	No	Some, especially 19 norsteroids and testosterone derivatives
Anabolic	No	Some
Thermogenic	Yes	Few mildly
Major metabolite	Pregnanediol	Not pregnanediol
Effect on foetus	Intellectual enhancement	Masculinisation of female if given in early pregnancy
Carcinogenic	None	Some carcinogenic to beagle dogs have been withdrawn

Many gynaecologists have been concerned by the recent increase in ectopic pregnancies which have occurred, and it has been suggested, but not confirmed, that this may be connected with the widespread use of progestogens.[3]

ORAL CONTRACEPTION

Progestogens are an essential component of the oral contraceptive pills, either in combination with oestrogen or as the progestogen-only pill. When it is appreciated that progestogen lowers the blood progesterone level, it is readily understood why sufferers of the premenstrual syndrome, who benefit when their progesterone blood level is raised, so often have difficulty in tolerating the Pill, which merely serves to increase the severity of their symptoms. In the hospital series of 100 consecutive patients, who had been referred for severe premenstrual syndrome, it was found that 44 women had used oral contraception of whom 40 (91%) had suffered from side effects, some stopping after only a few days.

As a 30-year-old mother wrote, "I have tried nine types of the Pill, but they all make me worse. After a few days I become cross, unhappy, anxious and emotional – at such times I find the baby's crying unbearable and just throw her into the cot if she won't shut up."

Another mother of two children wrote, "Every month for about three days after starting the Pill I get symptoms of depression and anxiety, lack of concentration and feel as if my metabolism is being thrown out of gear. I get muzzy heads, my thoughts are out of proportion and I cannot make decisions. Then suddenly I stop the Pills and it is as if something clicks into place and I feel well again for a few days."

Some women on oral contraceptives find that they remove the severe episode of premenstrual tension, by substituting a low grade depression throughout the month, and it is not until they stop the Pills for some other reason that they appreciate the general deterioration in their moods which occurred while on oral contraceptives. It is for this reason that many husbands have forbidden their wives to use the Pill.

References

1. Herst, A. L., Robboy, S. J., Macdonald, G. J., and Scully, R. (1975), *Amer. J. Obstet. Gynec.,* **118**, 607.
2. Johansson, E. D. B. (1971), *Acta Endocrin Kabenh.,* **66**, 799.
3. Liukkop and Erkkola (1976), *Brit. med. J.,* **2**, 1257.
4. Nillius, S. J., and Johansson, E. D. B. (1971), *Amer. J. Obstet. Gynec.,* **110**, 4, 470–477.

CHAPTER NINE

Progesterone Treatment

Not all patients with the premenstrual syndrome require progesterone treatment, which is expensive, and there is no justification in treating those whose symptoms do not warrant it. There are, however, many women whose symptoms not only warrant treatment but can only be relieved with progesterone.

Indications for Progesterone Treatment in the Premenstrual Syndrome

1. Where recurrent symptoms are interfering with the normal working capacity and life style.
2. Where there is a risk of premenstrual suicide, battering or alcoholism.
3. Where marital disharmony and domestic stress results from the symptoms.
4. Where costly hospital admission is the only alternative.

Other Indications for Progesterone Therapy

1. Cyclical symptoms at the menopause and in post-hysterectomy patients (Chapter 18).
2. Relief of pregnancy symptoms and the prophylaxis of pre-eclampsia (Chapter 15).
3. Threatened abortion, with a history of hyperemesis or pregnancy symptoms of increasing severity (Chapter 17).
4. Habitual abortion, where there is a history of hyperemesis or severe pregnancy symptoms preceding the previous spontaneous abortions (Chapter 17).
5. Puerperal depression (Chapter 16).
6. Prophylaxis of puerperal depression where there is a history of previous puerperal psychosis or depression (Chapter 16).
7. Treatment of stilboestrol-associated vaginal adenosis.[1]

Methods of Administration

There are five methods of administering progesterone:

1. Intramuscular injections (Chapter 11).
2. Suppositories (Chapter 10).
3. Pessaries (Chapter 10).
4. Implantation (Chapter 11).
5. Local application (page 83).

Dosage

Dosages of 25–100 mg daily may be used intra-muscularly, while the suppositories and pessaries are available in doses of 200 and 400 mg and may be used up to four times daily as their absorption is more rapid (Fig. 11.2). It is rarely necessary to increase the injections above 100 mg daily in the non-pregnant woman, although it may be raised to 300 mg daily during pregnancy or in the immediate post partum.

When pellets of pure progesterone are implanted five to twelve pellets of 25 or 100 mg may be used.

The dosage required tends to be higher among parous women, those of slim build and those with a history of pre-eclampsia, and does not appear to be related to age, severity or multiplicity of symptoms.

Following a pregnancy it will be necessary to re-establish the dose required. Women, who have had a good pregnancy and puerperium, may not need progesterone therapy again.

Overdose

Overdosage is almost impossible in a parous woman, who has already been exposed to considerably higher doses of progesterone for many months during pregnancy. In nulliparous women there may be euphoria, restless energy, insomnia, faintness and uterine cramps during menstruation. The presence of any of these is an indication for a reduction of the dose.

On rare occasions a generalised urticarial rash may appear following a progesterone injection. This appears to result from the oily solution, as these patients are able to tolerate suppositories or pessaries without a reaction.

Side Effects

Alterations to the cycle may be noted, usually with a reduction in the length, while in others menstruation may be postponed. Occasionally it may cause slight ovulatory bleeding if used during the follicular phase or premenstrual spotting. Usually the menstrual bleeding is lighter than normal. If a course of progesterone is started and then inadvertently stopped, menstruation will usually commence within 48 hours. This may happen when the patient has an unexpected weekend away from home, or if the nurse does not call on Sundays. Women, who are below the average weight for their height and age, may find that they gain weight on progesterone therapy. On the other hand, obese women often lose weight on progesterone.

In some women loss of libido may be noticed as a side effect, although in others progesterone restores libido.

Contra-indications

There are no contra-indications for the use of progesterone in the premenstrual syndrome, during pregnancy or in the puerperium.

Drug Interactions

No drug interactions have been noticed with progesterone. When progesterone is first given it is as well to leave the patient on any medication which she is already receiving, such as steroids, anti-convulsants, antidepressants, bronchodilators or diuretics, and then gradually reduce the other medication at the end of each course, eliminating the drug during the postmenstruum if it is being taken continuously. Progesterone can also be given simultaneously with progestogens, as in patients with endometriosis receiving nor-ethisterone.

Treatment of the Premenstrual Syndrome

It has already been emphasised that the diagnosis of the premenstrual syndrome depends on the time relationship of symptoms to menstruation and not on symptoms alone. Therefore it is essential before commencing treatment to have an accurate record of symptoms and menstruation (Chapter 2). There is a great temptation to start treatment on the evidence of a patient's verbal statement, especially if the symptoms are serious or urgent. Many patients have stated that their symptoms are premenstrual and that their menstruation has a regular cycle of 28 days with a three-day menstrual loss, only to find the following month that their symptoms extend until the second day of menstruation in a cycle of 32 days with five days' menstrual loss. Timing is critical and it is attention to these minor alterations in symptoms and cycles that determines the ideal course of treatment for an individual.

Initial Course

Progesterone has a cumulative action over the first five days of administration (Fig. 10.2), it is therefore wise to start the course of progesterone five days before symptoms are expected, although for ovulation symptoms it is only necessary to start two days earlier. The usual initial course is of 400 mg progesterone by suppository or pessary from Day 14 until the onset of menstruation.

If symptoms persist during menstruation treatment may be continued for the first few days of menstrual bleeding (Fig. 9.1).

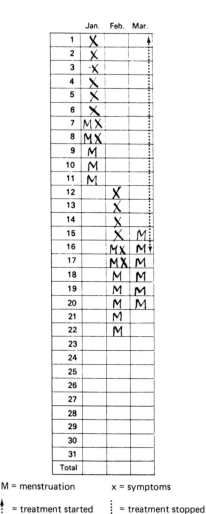

	Jan.	Feb.	Mar.
1	X		
2	X		
3	-X		
4	X		
5	X		
6	X		
7	M X		
8	M X		
9	M		
10	M		
11	M		
12		X	
13		X	
14		X	
15		X	M
16		M X	M
17		M X	M
18		M	M
19		M	M
20		M	M
21		M	
22		M	
23			
24			
25			
26			
27			
28			
29			
30			
31			
Total			

M = menstruation   x = symptoms

⁞ = treatment started   ⁞ = treatment stopped

Fig. 9.1   Initial course of progesterone from Day 14, continued until Day 2 as symptoms persisted until Day 2.

Patients, who have an unduly long cycle of 35 to 40 days with symptoms only on the last few days, should be given progesterone from Day 21 to 28. This will produce menstruation within 24–48 hours of stopping progesterone and thus before the symptoms would be expected (Fig. 9.2).

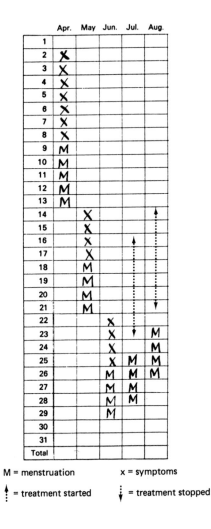

M = menstruation   x = symptoms

↑ = treatment started   ↓ = treatment stopped

Fig. 9.2 Long cycle of 39–40 days with symptoms on Days 34–40, treated with progesterone from Days 21–28 to shorten the cycle to 30 days and to eliminate symptoms.

Adjustments to the Course

After initial treatment adjustments may need to be made. Those who are symptom free may have the dose reduced to 200 mg suppositories or pessaries. The course may also be progressively reduced in gradations of two days from the initial course of 14 days to the shortest course which brings full symptomatic relief (Figure 9.3).

Patients who received partial benefit, noticing relief of symptoms during part of the day only, should be changed to twice daily administration of suppositories or pessaries. Others may have had relief of symptoms during the premenstruum, but with a postponement of symptoms during menstruation, and these should be given their normal dose during the premenstruum and half the dose during the first four days of menstruation.

Patients who receive no benefit from 400 mg suppositories or pessaries should have twice daily administration during the second month. If there is still no benefit a course of daily injections, 50 mg for nulliparous patient and 100 mg for parous patients, should be given. If daily injections bring relief, injections may then be given on alternate days.

After the initial course the patient may be given permission to use an extra suppository or pessary during the day if she feels the need, e.g. at times of mounting aggression, panic attacks, impending migraine or unaccountable depression. She should also be advised that if she stops the course prematurely menstruation is likely to follow within 48 hours of the last dose.

It might be mentioned that when treating blind patients, it is better not to aim at complete relief of all symptoms, for they usually prefer some mild symptoms as a warning of the imminence of menstruation, otherwise they may have difficulty in distinguishing a vaginal discharge from menstrual blood which could stain their clothing.

Duration

Women who have been incapacitated with premenstrual symptoms should first be allowed at least three months on the lowest dosage and shortest course on which they are symptom free before reducing the course still further. Then the course can be gradually reduced and stopped. When patients first stop progesterone there may be a period of about three months before the symptoms return to their original pretreatment severity. If symptoms recur each time the dose is reduced or the course shortened then the patient may need to continue indefinitely, or for a long period of time. At the menopause it is often possible to stop progesterone quite abruptly.

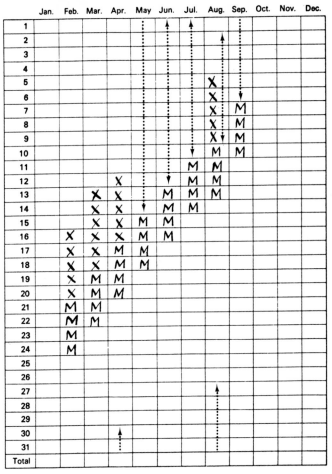

	Jan.	Feb.	Mar.	Apr.	May	Jun.	Jul.	Aug.	Sep.	Oct.	Nov.	Dec.
1						↑	↑					
2								↑				
3												
4												
5								X				
6								X	↓			
7								X	M			
8								X	M			
9								X ↓	M			
10							↓	M	M			
11							M	M				
12				X		↓	M	M				
13			X	X		M	M	M				
14			X	X	↓	M	M					
15			X	X	M	M						
16		X	X	X	M	M						
17		X	X	M	M							
18		X	X	M	M							
19		X	M	M								
20		X	M	M								
21		M	M									
22		M	M									
23		M										
24		M										
25												
26												
27							↑					
28												
29												
30				↑								
31												
Total												

M = menstruation   x = symptoms

↑ = treatment started   ↓ = treatment stopped

The initial course of progesterone from Day 14 until the
onset of menstruation eliminated symptoms. Subsequent
courses of 12 and 10 days also eliminated symptoms but
there was a return of symptoms on an 8-day course. Therefore subsequent treatment consisted of courses of 10 days
prior to menstruation.

Fig. 9.3 Progressive shortening of initial course of progesterone. All
symptoms were relieved on a 10-day course, but not on an 8-day
course.

Some patients, who have been able to stop progesterone and remain symptom free, may find that at times of stress they have a recurrence of symptoms and they will only need temporary progesterone treatment.

There does not seem to be any risk of developing tolerance to progesterone and there is no addiction.

Long-term Effects

There are 40 women, who have been on continuous progesterone therapy, and under constant surveillance, for over 10 years. No adverse effects have been noted in these women, although a raised glucose tolerance curve was found in a few of them, particularly among those with amenorrhoea following an implant or after a hysterectomy, but there have been no cases of diabetes in these, or in any progesterone-treated women during the past 20 years. The 28-year-old mother with premenstrual epilepsy, whose chart was shown in Fig. 5.3, had an oral glucose tolerance test (dose 1 gm/kg = 72·6 gm) before commencing progesterone treatment. These tests were repeated over the following two years and the last one showed mildly abnormal glucose levels (Fig. 9.4).

Conception

Those anxious to conceive should start progesterone administration on Day 16, or if they are recording their basal temperature, the day following ovulation. They should then be advised to continue progesterone until the pregnancy has been confirmed.

Contraception

Patients with the premenstrual syndrome usually have difficulty in tolerating the oestrogen-progestogen or the progestogen-only pill, probably because the progestogen lowers the plasma progesterone level. If they have difficulty or strong objections to other contraceptive measures, then after the optimum course of progesterone has been found, progesterone should be started on a low dose, e.g. 100 mg daily by suppository from Day 8 until Day 13, and the normal dose used from Day 14 until the onset of menstruation. This is contraceptively safe but in some women the early administration of progesterone results in breakthrough bleeding on Days 16–20. In this latter group the woman may use norethisterone 0·5 mg, as in the progestogen-only pill, from Day 5 until 14 and then use progesterone in the normal way.

The intra-uterine device which slowly releases progesterone to the endometrium can be a useful form of contraception for sufferers of the

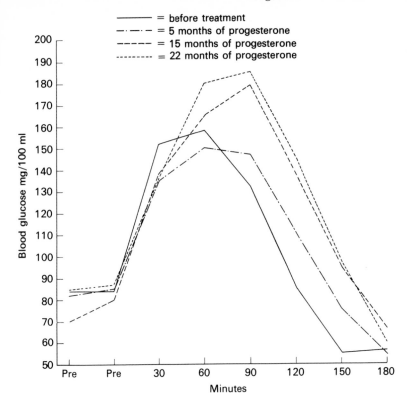

Fig. 9.4   Glucose Tolerance Curves before and after progesterone treatment in a 28-year-old patient with premenstrual epilepsy.

premenstrual syndrome, but the small dose of progesterone has no therapeutic value.

Individual Tailoring

It will be appreciated that the course and dose of progesterone is individually tailored for each patient. This is not surprising in view of the innumerable presentations, differences in precise timing of symptoms, variation in lengths of the menstrual cycle and desire for conception or contraception. The optimum treatment schedule of 100 consecutive hospital patients suffering from severe premenstrual syndrome is shown in Table 9.1.

Table 9.1

Optimum Progesterone Treatment of 100 Consecutive

Hospital Patients

Dose	Suppositories or pessaries		
	100 mg die		1
	200 mg die		9
	200 mg b.d.		1
	400 mg die		34
	400 mg b.d.		21
	400 mg t.d.s.		7
	400 mg p.r.n.		2
		Total	*75*
	Injections		
	50 mg alt. die		1
	75 mg die		1
	100 mg die		5
	100 mg alt. die		2
		Total	*9*
	Implant		
	10 × 100 mg		2
		Total	*2*
	Symptom free, treatment stopped		14

Day of menstrual cycle for commencing progesterone

Day	8	3	
	10	6	
	12	10	
	14	44	
	16	2	
	18	4	
	20	4	
	22	2	
Continuously		7	(menopausal)
When necessary		2	
	Total	*84*	

Failure to Respond

Failure of patients with the premenstrual syndrome to respond to progesterone treatment is either due to (1) incorrect diagnosis or (2) incorrect frequency or dosage.

When faced with a patient with incapacitating symptoms, which she claims are related to menstruation, it is a great temptation to commence progesterone treatment without a definitive menstrual record, especially in those who may have travelled a considerable distance or may have waited weeks for an appointment. A business executive of 40 years brought a doctor's letter stating she had "a clear history of premenstrual migraine". She was first seen during menstruation and stated she had been incapacitated by migraine on six of the previous eight days, but she did not have a menstrual record. She was started on progesterone suppositories which brought no relief, however, after two months it was clear from her menstrual chart and her completed attack forms that the symptoms were not related to menstruation. She did not have a phase free from migraine during the cycle and her migraine proved to be caused by certain foods in her diet.

If the menstrual record and history confirm the diagnosis of the premenstrual syndrome, then one is justified in raising the daily injection dose to 100 mg from Day 14 until the onset of menstruation before regarding the patient as failing to respond. There are variations in the rate and completeness of rectal and vaginal absorption of progesterone and for some the effect of progesterone is too shortlived, and they may need intra-muscular injections.

Local Progesterone

There are a few instances where local progesterone may be used with good effect, but in most cases the patients are polysymptomatic and warrant systemic treatment. Nasal drops 10% may be used in the treatment of premenstrual rhinitis, and progesterone cream 10% may be used for premenstrual vaginal and vulval ulceration. In both cases the local pharmacist will need to prepare the preparation. Progesterone gel is available in France and recommended for premenstrual mastitis.

References

1. Herbet, A. L., Robboy, S. J., Macdonald, G. J., and Scully, R. E. (1974), *Amer. J. Obstet. Gynec.*, March, 607.

CHAPTER TEN

Progesterone Suppositories and Pessaries

Progesterone is a white crystalline powder, which is dissolved in inert wax to form suppositories or pessaries, the same preparation being used for either the rectal or vaginal route. The wax has a low melting point, as several women have discovered when travelling in hot countries. Their shelf life is two years. Their great advantage is that of self-administration. and for this reason suppositories and pessaries are surprisingly well accepted by most women, particularly if their symptoms are severe.

Nillius and Johansson[2] studied the pattern of rectal absorption after the administration of 25 mg and 100 mg progesterone in two groups of women of fertile age during the follicular phase. Peak plasma levels of progesterone were obtained at 4 to 8 hours after administration, followed by a gradual decline. It should be noted that one of the subjects, who received 25 mg, showed only an insignificant increase in plasma progesterone (Fig. 10.1).

One woman was studied by Nillius and Johansson during the follicular phase following the rectal administration of 100 mg progesterone at 24-hour intervals for five days, and they also obtained the plasma progesterone levels at 12 and 24 hours. They found it was not possible to maintain a stable elevated plasma level of progesterone with this dosage although there was a tendency to a cumulative effect during the five days of treatment (Fig. 10.2). They noted that the rise and fall in plasma progesterone levels coincided with pronounced "early pregnancy symptoms" such as nausea and depression.

Nillius and Johansson also studied the plasma levels of progesterone following the vaginal administration of 100 mg of progesterone to six women of fertile age during the follicular phase. There was a rapid increase in plasma levels of progesterone reaching a peak within 4 hours and gradually falling during the following 8 hours, although after 24 hours three of the women still had a plasma level of progesterone above the level normally found in the follicular phase of the menstrual cycle (Fig. 10.3).

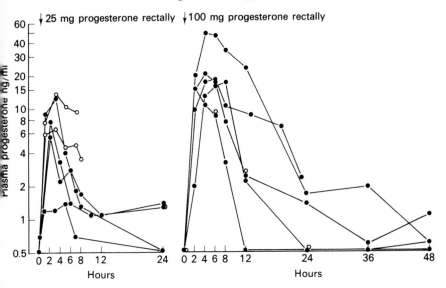

Fig. 10.1 Plasma levels of progesterone after rectal administration of two groups of six women in the follicular phase of the menstrual cycle. (From Nillius, S. J., and Johansson, E. D. B. (1971), *Amer. J. Obs. Gynaec.*, 110, 4, 470.)

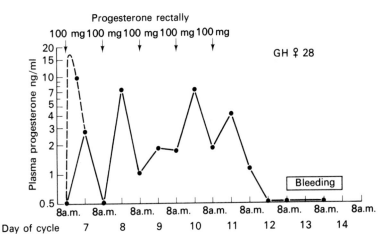

Fig. 10.2 Plasma levels of progesterone before, during and after five days of daily rectal administration of 100 mg progesterone to a woman in the follicular phase of the menstrual cycle. (From Nillius, S. J., and Johansson, E. D. B. (1971), *Amer. J. Obs. Gynaec.*, 110, 4, 470.)

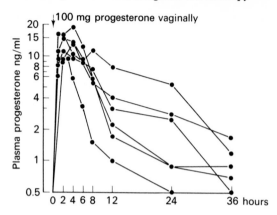

Fig. 10.3   Plasma levels of progesterone after vaginal administration of 100 mg progesterone to six women in the follicular phase of the menstrual cycle. (From Nillius, S. J. and Johansson, E. D. B. (1971), *Amer. J. Obs. Gynaec.*, 110, 4, 470.)

Clinical observation would support these findings of Nillius and Johansson as regards the short duration of action of rectal absorption, the finding of some patients in whom there is poor rectal absorption and the beneficial effect of the cumulative action which is manifested after several days' treatment. For this reason it is frequently necessary to administer suppositories and pessaries two to four times daily, and to start treatment five days before the expected onset of symptoms.

There is considerable individual variation in the absorption patterns and they estimated that approximately four times the injection dose is required to produce the same rise in plasma level of progesterone as that obtained by the rectal or vaginal route.

In practice suppositories and pessaries are interchangeable and it is left to the individual to decide on the route. There are cultural variations which determine the choice, while some women use both routes alternatively. With vaginal administration there is no effective sphincter to control the leakage of wax, so some women use this route at night when soiling of underclothes is not such a problem, and use the rectal route in the morning. Yet others prefer the pessaries in the morning so as not to interfere with the habitual morning opening of the bowels. Patients are advised that if they defaecate within an hour of the insertion of a suppository another one should be used.

Permission is given to patients to use an extra suppository or pessary during the day if they feel the need, such as an impending migraine, sudden onset of tiredness, depression or irritability, or wheezing, and at times of stress. Patients soon learn their own requirements and the time interval which suits them best.

Some women have observed that if they use half a 400 mg suppository instead of a whole 200 mg the problem of wax leakage is decreased.

Side Effects

Anal soreness, diarrhoea and flatulence may occur with the suppositories. In cases of anal soreness the patient may be advised to use a bland ointment at the time of insertion. Following the use of pessaries patients may complain of a vaginal discharge, which is the leakage of the inert wax. Poor vaginal absorption is often found following a total hysterectomy.

Contra-indications

Suppositories should be avoided in those with a history of colitis and faecal incontinence. Pessaries are contra-indicated in those with vaginal infection, especially moniliasis, and in those with recurrent cystitis.

Comparison of Effectiveness of Injections with Suppositories and Pessaries

Controlled trials into the prophylactic value of progesterone injections in pre-eclampsia[1] were later repeated using the same protocol but with

Table 10.1

Comparison of Progesterone Injections and Suppositories and Pessaries

| | Progesterone | | Controls | |
| | | Suppositories or | | Suppositories or |
	Injections	pessaries	Injections	pessaries
Number in Group	62	80	66	88
	%	%	%	%
Pre-eclampsia	3*	3*	11	11
B.P. over 140/90	11*	11	20	19
Oedema	4*	6*	17	18
Albuminuria	2	–*	7	7

* = Probability < 0·05

suppositories or pessaries instead. The dosage used was the lowest which would control the pregnancy symptoms in each individual. The results of the trials showed a remarkable similarity in action (Table 10.1).

References

1. Dalton, K. (1962), *J. Obstet. Gynec.,* **69**, 3.
2. Nillius, S. J., and Johansson, E. D. B. (1971), *Amer. J. Obstet. Gynec.,* **110**, 4, 470.

CHAPTER ELEVEN

Progesterone Injections and Implantation

Progesterone is insoluble in water but soluble in alcohol, arachis oil, chloroform and ether. The B.P. preparation of progesterone is dissolved in ethyl oleate. Very occasionally solid matter separates out on prolonged standing in the cold, should this occur it may be dissolved by slowly heating the ampule.

Indications for Progesterone Injections

1. Failure to respond to suppositories or pessaries.
2. Where suppositories and pessaries are contra-indicated or/and disliked by the patient.
3. Hospitalised patients.
4. Those requiring daily supervision from a nurse, as where there is a risk of suicide, battering or alcoholic bout.

Duration of Action

Nillius and Johansson[1] studied eight menstruating women in the follicular phase of the cycle and four postmenopausal women following an intramuscular injection of 100 mg progesterone and found a peak level was usually obtained within 8 hours, and elevated levels persisted for up to 48 hours in most subjects (Fig. 11.1).

They also found the elevation of plasma progesterone proportional to the dose administered. One woman volunteered for five experiments during a one-year period, and it was possible to determine the effectiveness of various doses and routes of administration (Fig. 11.2).

The studies of Nillius and Johansson confirm the clinical observation that progesterone injections need to be given daily or at least on alternate days. Some women, particularly those receiving treatment for the relief of pregnancy symptoms, notice that if given injections on alternate days, they have alternate symptomatic and symptom free days.

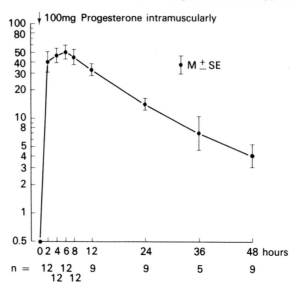

Fig. 11.1 The mean plasma level of progesterone after intramuscular administration of 100 mg progesterone to eight women in the follicular phase of the menstrual cycle and four postmenopausal women. (From Nillius, S. J., and Johansson, E. D. B. (1971), *Amer. J. Obs. Gynaec.*, 110, 4, 470.)

Administration

Progesterone injections require a site where there is ample fat so that a depot of progesterone can be formed for release into the blood, therefore injections should be given deep into the buttock rather than into the thigh or deltoid. A $1\frac{1}{2}$ inch (3·8 cm) needle should be used, as too superficial an injection may cause soreness and possible urticaria. It is wise to use one needle for drawing up the solution and another for injections, to avoid infiltration of the dermis by progesterone or solvent on the surface of the needle. The soreness which may result from an injection appears to be more the property of the solvent than the active ingredient, for during controlled trials when patients were injected at random with either progesterone or the solvent only, it was found that as many complaints of soreness at the injection site arose from those receiving the solvent only as from those receiving progesterone.

Initially the injections may be given by the practice, district or factory nurse, but with suitable instruction most patients soon learn the art of giving their own injections. Failing this the husbands may be ready to learn

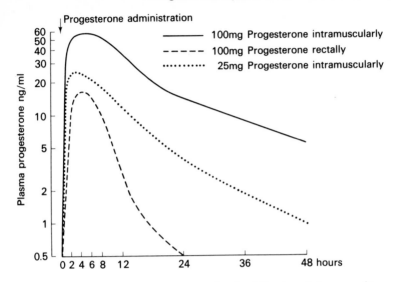

Fig. 11.2 Plasma progesterone levels following intramuscular injections and rectal administration. (From Nillius, S. J., and Johansson, E. D. B. (1971), *Amer. J. Obs. Gynaec.*, 110, 4, 470.)

the technique. The use of an injection gun gives many patients the necessary initial confidence for self-injection. For women at risk during the premenstruum the daily visit of a nurse to give the injection is a valuable form of silent supervision.

Dosage

Progesterone injections are available in ampules of 25 mg, 50 mg and 100 mg. In the non-pregnant woman it is rarely necessary to exceed 100 mg daily, but during pregnancy, when the progesterone levels are considerably raised, doses of 100 mg can be given three times daily.

As previously mentioned, following an intramuscular injection some women experience the characteristic taste of progesterone within three minutes of injection. This is due to the rapid metabolism, with some of the metabolites being excreted via the lungs. These women are always the ones who obtain positive benefit from progesterone and are usually those who require daily injections.

Side Effects

Some women develop an abscess after several months or years of progesterone injections. It is common among those who give their own injections, repeatedly using the same site, or inject using too short a needle. The abscess is caused by unabsorbed oil, it is deep seated and sterile; however, it may remain unresolved and need incision and drainage. If the buttock is hot or inflamed injections should not be given, suppositories or pessaries must be used as alternatives.

IMPLANTATION

Compressed pellets of pure progesterone may be implanted into the fat of the anterior abdominal wall. This method obviates the necessity of frequent injections, suppositories or pessaries.

Indications for Implantation

1. Women who have had complete relief of symptoms on progesterone injections, suppositories or pessaries.
2. Those still having cyclical symptoms after the menopause or hysterectomy.
3. Erratic users of progesterone, such as the feckless alcoholics.

One patient living in Italy calculated that the cost of an annual implant plus the air fare from Rome was cheaper than the cost of daily suppositories.

Contra-indications

1. Those wishing to conceive within twelve months. A progesterone implant inhibits ovulation for many months.
2. Those unduly concerned by irregular menstruation, scanty loss or spells of amenorrhoea which may last about six months.
3. Those who must avoid premenstrual symptoms at all cost, e.g. epileptics, for they may not appreciate when their implanted supply of progesterone is coming to an end and may have an attack at a most unfortunate and potentially dangerous time.
4. Those whose progesterone requirement is too high, i.e. above 75 mg injection daily, or 400 mg t.d.s. of suppository or pessary.

Preliminary Precautions

To diminish the possibility of extrusion of the pellets one should ensure that the patient has had regular progesterone during the five days immediately prior to implantation, and that the woman is either still menstruating or in the immediate postmenstruum.

Dosage

Pellets of 25 mg and 100 mg progesterone are available. The usual dose for a non-pregnant woman is five to twelve pellets of 100 mg. As several pellets are required, a progesterone implant is not as easy to perform as an oestrogen implant at the menopause.

Duration

The duration of action of an implant may vary between 3 and 12 months. Some patients find that repeated implants all have the same duration of action, while in others it may vary for no obvious reason. An investigation into the duration of effectiveness of an implant given to 77 patients with the premenstrual syndrome failed to reveal any significant factor. The duration did not appear to be related to the type of symptoms or their timing in regard to menstruation, the presence or absence of much bleeding or bruising at the implant site, the batch number of the progesterone pellets, the tendency to extrusion, the depth of abdominal fat or the presence or absence of pain at the implant site.

The end of the effectiveness of an implant is usually very gradual with a return of tension symptoms before the somatic symptoms of migraine, epilepsy or asthma return. Frequently it is the husband who first notices, by his wife's bad temper, that the time for further treatment has come.

Requirements for Implantation

1. Pellets of progesterone
2. Local anaesthetic
3. Scalpel
4. Trocar and canular
5. Suture material
6. Skin marking pencil

Method

It is convenient to mark the skin radially from the proposed incision to show where the pellets are to be implanted, and to ensure that the local anaesthetic penetrates those areas. Under a local anaesthetic a 1 cm incision is made into the skin of the anterior abdominal wall, the canular is inserted deep into the fat and using the trocar the pellets are embedded into the fat to the full extent of the canular (Fig. 11.3) If more than six pellets are being used two pellets may be embedded at the same site. One suture or clip is usually all that is required.

Subsequently there may be some tenderness or bruising for a few days in the slim patients, but the obese are usually surprisingly free from pain. The following week the pellets may be felt as round masses or as one patient described it "like a sack of new potatoes".

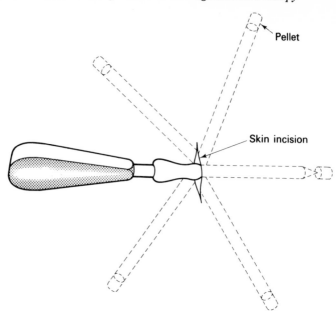

Fig. 11.3   Method of progesterone implantation.

Extrusion of Pellets

Extrusion of pellets are more likely to occur when they are not implanted in fat (e.g. into the thigh or fascia lata) when the implant is performed during the premenstruum or in a patient already depleted of progesterone. After each implantation the patient should be advised that if the site becomes red or tender she should have 100 mg progesterone intramuscularly for five consecutive days. Prior to an extrusion the site may become red and tender at each premenstruum for two or more cycles subsiding in the interval, and then finally extruding in the premenstruum. Extrusions have been known to occur as early as two weeks and as late as sixteen months after implantation, and are rare in pregnancy. The pellet is usually extruded through a punched-out hole which heals rapidly.

Side Effects

Insomnia or restless energy may be noted for the first few days, and it may be necessary to give mild sedation, but this requirement rarely lasts long.

The scar of a progesterone implant may develop brown pigmentation during a subsequent pregnancy.

Reference

1. Nillius, S. J., and Johansson, E. D. B. (1971), *Amer. J. Obstet. Gynec.*, **110**, 4, 470.

CHAPTER TWELVE

Alternative Treatment

The premenstrual syndrome has a very individual but specific presentation in each woman, which needs careful and personal consideration because of the variety of symptoms and their severity; the variations in cycle length and duration of menstruation; the age, parity, occupation and domestic circumstances all need evaluating. Alternative treatment is suitable for two types of patients, those whose premenstrual syndrome is mild and readily responsive to symptomatic treatment, and those who are still completing a menstrual chart to confirm the diagnosis.

REASSURANCE OF MENSTRUAL CHART

Encouraging the patient to record the dates of symptoms and menstruation for a few months is always worth while. This reassures the patient, as she sees for herself, that although the chronic symptoms recur there is always a phase free from symptoms in each cycle. Too often her visit to the doctor is accompanied by a hidden fear that the joint pains are an early sign of crippling arthritis, or that the headaches doom her to a painful death from a cerebral tumour. A chart may be particularly useful for the women with recurrent upper respiratory infection who is demanding monthly supplies of antibiotics. Once the allergic, and non-infectious nature of her rhinitis is appreciated she may be able to accept a prophylactic course of mild antihistamine drugs.

SELF-HELP TREATMENT

Once the patient recognises that she has mild premenstrual syndrome she should be taught to adjust her life style to the cyclical indisposition. It should be explained to her that during the premenstruum she should avoid long shopping trips, exhausting outings, heavy washdays and other heavy household tasks, instead she should enjoy the invitations to tea or dinner and tackle the darning or light sewing. The woman will also need reassuring that after menstruation she will have all the energy she needs to do the work that she had left undone during the premenstruum.

She should also aim to have extra rest with earlier bedtimes, and spells of relaxation during the day. Today many young mothers have learnt the art of relaxation for childbirth and can use these exercises at home. She may prefer to do this alone at home or to join one of the "Relaxation for Living" classes locally. The restriction of fluid intake to one pint daily and the limitation of the salt has advantages for those with marked water retention. It is surprising how many women spend all day drinking tea or coffee during the premenstruum mistakenly hoping it will give them a little more energy.

Constipation is an almost universal accompaniment of the premenstrual syndrome and simple correction is beneficial. In India there is a custom for all women to take a dose of magnesium sulphate during the premenstruum to relieve the body of accumulated poisons. It is fascinating to find how often ancient customs turn out to be of value, although not always in the way that the ancients envisaged it. There is much to commend their use of magnesium sulphate as both a laxative and a dehydrating agent.

The realisation that many symptoms result from hypoglycaemia during the premenstruum suggests that sufferers should be warned not to go for too long an interval without food during the premenstruum and to avoid too drastic dieting at this time. They should be advised to always have a breakfast, even if it is a low calorie one. At the eleven o'clock break and in the afternoon an apple and cheese is better than a cup of tea, and if supper is taken early it is important to have a bedtime snack.

Women in whom there is any suspicion that the Pill is increasing the premenstrual syndrome should be advised to try an alternative method of contraception. Chapter 8 explained why the oral contraceptive Pill is likely to accentuate any premenstrual symptoms.

The previous treatment given to 100 consecutive hospital patients with severe premenstrual syndrome is shown in Table 12.1. It is interesting that the tranquillisers and anti-depressants failed to ease the symptoms adequately. Today there are doctors still giving amphetamine drugs for chronic recurrent symptoms and to the very patients most likely to become habituated.

PROGESTOGENS

Chapter 8 dealt with the differences between progesterone and progestogens, and explained how most of the actions required of progesterone in the treatment of premenstrual syndrome were not present

Table 12.1

Previous Treatment of 100 Consecutive Hospital Patients

Tranquillisers	39
Anti-depressants	29
Diuretics	17
Progestogens	13
Oral contraceptive pills	13
Amphetamine	3
Analgesics	3

(Some patients are included in more than one category)

in progestogens. Progestogens should NOT be regarded as routine treatment for the premenstrual syndrome; however, there are a few conditions in which they can be used beneficially.

Patients, whose presenting symptoms are engorged and tender breasts premenstrually, often benefit from the androgenic progestogens, such as nor-ethisterone in doses of 5–15 mg daily from ovulation to the onset of menstruation. If necessary diuretics may be given simultaneously. Post-hysterectomy patients with cyclical lower abdominal pains, and possibly a history of endometriosis, may benefit from continuous nor-ethisterone 10–30 mg daily in courses of six months with a gradual reduction over the year (page 112).

Those suffering from congestive dysmenorrhoea, who have mild premenstrual tension, but in whom the presenting symptom is premenstrual lower abdominal pain, increasing in severity until the onset of menstruation may benefit from dydrogesterone 10–30 mg daily in courses starting either from Day 5 or Day 14 and continuing until menstruation.

Medroxyprogesterone is helpful for those with premenstrual symptoms exacerbated at times of food depletion, such as the woman who develops headaches after she has been working five or more hours without nourishment, the housewife complaining of overwhelming exhaustion when preparing the evening meal, or the mother with outbursts of irritability when the children come home late from school. Medroxyprogesterone raises the glucose tolerance so it is contra-indicated in those with a diabetic family history. It is given in doses of 5 to 15 mg from ovulation to menstruation.

DIURETICS

Diuretics are a simple method of helping the patient with mild premenstrual symptoms that are due to water retention, but they will not help the psychological symptoms, and indeed they may increase the lethargy. Therefore the choice should be one of the slower acting potassium-sparing diuretics, preferably used on alternate days, from ovulation to menstruation. If only partial benefit is obtained, there is a natural temptation to increase the dosage and frequency, and to change to the quick-acting diuretics, the course then gets extended and electrolyte imbalance occurs. By this time the patient is often addicted to them and claims that she gets bloatedness if they are stopped only for one day. As one patient explained, "But I can even hear the water splashing about in my stomach."

Potassium

Potassium depletion may be suspected in those giving a history of prolonged diuretic administration, food cravings, prolonged dieting, and who complain of lethargy and muscle weakness throughout the cycle. Potassium, either as effervescent or enteric coated tablets, should be given sufficient to maintain the potassium level above the lower level of normal.

Spironolactone

It was hoped that spironolactone, an aldosterone antagonist, would prove helpful in this syndrome, but these hopes have not been fulfilled in practice. If used, it is best given as the combination tablet with a diuretic, and although it is claimed to be potassium-sparing it is well to have regular potassium estimations done and give a potassium supplement if indicated.

ANTI-DEPRESSANTS

Anti-depressants would appear to be the first line of treatment for the premenstrual depression, but in practice it is among this group of women that most of the failures are noticed, possibly because tricyclic anti-depressants raise the prolactin level. Doses of tricyclics, which are effective in other patients, tend to increase the premenstrual lethargy and therefore makes them unacceptable. The tricyclic group take about two weeks to have their full effect, which means that if they are used they should be given during the symptom free two weeks in the hope of helping the two depressed weeks. For premenstrual depressives, lithium is the most useful drug for easing the mood swings and the depression, and can be used with progesterone if necessary.

Bromocriptine

Bromocriptine is the most recent drug advocated for the treatment of premenstrual syndrome.[1] Its place in lowering prolactin levels is undisputed and it has proved effective in amenorrhoea/galactorrhoea syndrome and in the inhibition of lactation. In premenstrual syndrome it has been most successful where there is breast engorgement and generalised oedema, and in those with a recent history of puerperal depression in whom it may bring relief regardless of whether or not the prolactin levels are raised. The side effects include nausea and vomiting (particularly if taken without food), headaches, insomnia, confusion and an increase in libido. The usual dose is 2·5 mg bromocriptine daily from Day 10 until the onset of menstruation. This dose can then gradually be increased by monthly increments up to 7·5 mg. In patients already on progesterone therapy it can be started gradually, initially with progesterone, and then gradually reducing the progesterone while increasing the bromocriptine.

Recent double-blind controlled trials in 13 patients using 2·5 mg bromocriptine or identical placebo tablets failed to show any significant difference in the alleviation of premenstrual mood swings, swelling or headaches.[2]

Pyridoxine

Pyridoxine is helpful in a small proportion of women who develop premenstrual depression following the use of the oral contraceptive pill, and may be given as a therapeutic trial in doses of 20–50 mg t.d.s. If no benefit accrues within one cycle it should be discontinued.

Reference

1. Benedek-Jaszmann, L. J., and Hearn-Sturtevant, M. D. (1976), *Lancet*, **1**, 1095.
2. Ghose, K., and Coppen, A. (1977), *Brit. med. J.*, **1**, 148.

CHAPTER THIRTEEN

Adjustment of Menstruation

The deleterious effects of the premenstrual syndrome are described in Chapters 4, 5, 19 and 20. The time of risk is invariably the paramenstruum with relative freedom from these disturbances during other phases of the cycle and indeed, an increased sense of well being in the postmenstruum. The extent to which these paramenstrual influences have a prejudicial effect upon the sufferer is a very individual matter. The adjustment of menstruation to avoid those deleterious effects, at times when the patient requires to be at the peak of her abilities, can be fully justified.

With our greater understanding of the menstrual hormones, adjustment of menstruation is now a practical proposition, and in fact this is exactly what happens when a woman goes on the oestrogen-progestogen contraceptive pill. However, the mere postponement of menstruation which allows a prolongation of the incapacitating premenstrual symptoms is of no value.

It must be emphasised that not all women are handicapped by menstruation. There are those who have anovular cycles, following a period of amenorrhoea, and these women are usually remarkably free from paramenstrual symptoms.

Adjustment of menstruation has been requested by students, sportswomen and actresses in respect of specific occasions such as examinations, interviews, competitions or performances. The event may only last a single day or be continuous over a period of three or more weeks. It may be a request purely for social convenience as for a wedding, or a holiday jet flight.

A prerequisite to the adjustment of menstruation is an accurate menstrual chart with a known date of the event on which menstruation is to be avoided. In this respect there is a vital difference between a cycle of 28 days and one of 31 days, for after an interval of only a couple of cycles there would be a six-day difference in regard to the event. All too often the woman announces she has a regular cycle of 28 days, to which a convenient question may be posed, "What day of the week does your period occur?" Only if it is precisely regular will she be able to state the day spontaneously. It is also useful to have some idea of the phase in the cycle of her best performances, which again varies individually. It is often best between Days 9–12 and 17–21, but some sportswomen are surprised to find that they perform best during their aggressive premenstrual phase. Students whose essays are marked weekly, and sportswomen, who do a daily time check in training, may be able to give these particulars with

	Jan.	Feb.	Mar.	Apr.
1				
2		✓		✓
3				
4				
5	✓			
6		✓		
7		✓		
8				
9			✓	
10				
11				
12			✓	
13			✓	
14	✳			
15	✳			✓
16	M ✳			✓
17	M			
18	M			
19	M	✳		
20	M	✳		
21		M		
22		M		
23		M	✳M	✳
24	✓	M	M	✳
25	✓		M	M
26			M	M
27			M	M
28			M	M
29				M
30			✓	
31				
Total				

M, menstruation; ✓, good performance; ✳, poor performance.

Fig. 13.1 Performance and menstruation. (From *Sports Medicine*, Williams, J. G. P., and Sperryn, P. N. London; E. Arnold.)

accuracy. Fig. 13.1 shows the dates of good and poor performance during the training programme of a sportswoman.

The drugs available to alter menstruation are oestrogens, progestogens, and progesterone. Any one of these, if given after ovulation for a few days and then stopped, may be expected to cause menstruation or withdrawal bleeding within 48 hours of cessation.

OESTROGENS

Oestrogens are of value in the teenager who has immature sexual development or who suffers from spasmodic dysmenorrhoea. The side effects of oestrogen administration can be nausea, headache, weight gain and depression. Oestrogen may be conveniently given as ethinyl oestradiol in doses of 10–50 µg daily, or may be given with a progestogen as in the oral oestrogen-progestogen contraceptive pill.

PROGESTOGENS

Progestogens are useful for those with irregular and anovular menstruation. The 19 nor-steroids are best, used in a dose of 5 mg or as an oral oestrogen-progestogen contraceptive pill.

PROGESTERONE

Progesterone is best for those with premenstrual syndrome, congestive dysmenorrhoea or with a tendency to suffer from bloatedness, weight gain, headaches or mood swings.

Method

The easiest cycles to adjust are those of women who are already on oral contraceptives, for the course can easily be extended or contracted and the time of menstruation reliably predicted. Furthermore, these women already know how soon bleeding starts after they have taken their last Pill.

Ideally, if one is adjusting for a specific event it is best to adjust the cycles in the month beforehand so that no medication need be given in the month of the event. Fig. 13.2 shows the chart of a sportswoman who had noted poor performances in the late premenstruum and early menstruation during February to April. The cycle in May was shortened to 21 days by giving an oestrogen-progestogen pill from Day 5–19. The next two menstruations occurred at their normal interval, allowing the woman to perform during her optimum phase of the postmenstruum.

	Jan.	Feb.	Mar.	Apr.	May	Jun.	Jul.
1							M
2							M
3						M	M
4						M	
5						M	
6					M	M	
7					M		
8					M		
9							C
10							
11							
12				M			
13				M			
14				M			
15			M	M			
16		M	M				
17		M	M				
18	M	M					
19	M	M					
20	M						
21	M						
22							
23							
24							
25							
26							
27							
28							
29							
30							
31							
Total							

The menstrual cycle in May was shortened. Normal menstruation occurred in June and July. M, menstruation; C, competition; ▲, treatment started; ⋮, treatment stopped.

Fig. 13.2   Adjusting menstruation in a woman with a regular cycle. (From *Sports Medicine*, Williams, J. G. P., and Sperryn, P. N. London: E. Arnold.)

On the other hand, the sportswoman whose chart is shown in Fig. 13.3 also had her poorest performances in the premenstruum, but had an irregular cycle varying from 26–35 days. The menstrual cycle was shortened in May to 21 days by the administration of an oestrogen-progestogen pill from Days 5–19; but to ensure against the possibility of a

	Jan.	Feb.	Mar.	Apr.	May	Jun.	Jul.
1					:	↑	M
2					:	:	M
3					:	↓	M
4					:		M
5					:	M	
6					↓	M	
7						M	
8					M	M	
9					M		C
10					M		
11					M		
12							
13			M				
14			M				
15		M	M				
16		M	M				
17		M		M			
18	M			M			
19	M			M			
20	M			M			
21	M			↑			
22				:			
23				:			
24				:			
25				:			
26				:			
27				:			
28				:		↑	
29				:		:	
30				:		↓	
31							
Total							

Cycle length varies from 26 to 35 days. The menstrual cycle in May was shortened to 21 days. The June and July cycles were regularized with short 3-day courses of treatment. M, menstruation; C, competition; ↑, treatment started; ↓, treatment stopped.

Fig. 13.3 Adjusting menstruation in a woman with an irregular cycle. (From *Sports Medicine*, Williams, J. G. P., and Sperryn, P. N. London: E. Arnold.)

long cycle in June or July a three-day course of the Pill was also given on Days 24–26 in June.

Inevitably one is also consulted by those who attend too late to properly adjust their cycle. The candidate in Fig. 13.4 attended only nine days before the competition, which did not provide enough time in which to give the minimum of a three-day course of medication, to allow 48 hours for bleeding to occur and to have completed menstruation before the

	Jan.	Feb.	Mar.	Apr.	May	Jun.	Jul.
1							↑
2							
3							
4							
5							
6							
7						M	
8			M		M	M	
9			M	M	M	M	C
10			M	M	M	M	↓
11			M	M	M	M	
12			M	M	M	M	M
13			M	M	M	M	M
14			M	M	M	M	M
15				M			M
16							M
17							M
18							M
19							
20							
21							
22							
23							
24							
25							
26							
27							
28							
29							
30							
31							
Total							

Late consultation only 9 days before event, treated with progesterone. Although progestogens will delay menstruation they will not prevent premenstrual deterioration of performance. M, menstruation; C, competition; ↑, treatment started; ↓, treatment stopped.

Fig. 13.4   Late adjustment of menstruation. (From *Sports Medicine* Williams, J. G. P., and Sperryn, P. N. London: E. Arnold.)

competition. So instead she was given a nine-day course of progesterone suppositories 400 mg to use each morning until after the competition, this prevented premenstrual deterioration and postponed menstruation (Fig. 13.4).

If it is desired to shorten the cycle by only two or three days or if menstruation is already overdue then medication need only be given for three days to be successful. However, if it is desired to shorten the cycle to 16 days, then medication needs to be given continuously from Day 5 until Day 14. Progestogens may be given in this case, even to sufferers of the premenstrual syndrome, as there is no risk that they will reduce the blood progesterone level, which is absent during the follicular phase.

There may be a demand for a longer suppression of menstruation, as with an actress who may have a continuous programme of events for a few months. In this case oestrogens, progestogens, or progesterone may be used continuously, and although there may be the occasional breakthrough bleeding this is usually scanty, free from symptoms and does not affect performance. The dose should be the lowest compatible with suppression for each individual, and this can often be lowered at monthly intervals. Sufferers from spasmodic dysmenorrhoea, in particular, will benefit from such a regime and may be free from dysmenorrhoea when it is decided to resume normal menstruation. Work is proceeding on a contraceptive pill to be administered in courses of two and three months in which menstruation will occur at these longer intervals.

CHAPTER FOURTEEN

Dysmenorrhoea

Women who complain of pain with menstruation, and in whom a full physical and gynaecological examination reveals no abnormality, can be divided into two types:

1. *Spasmodic dysmenorrhoea*, sometimes called idiopathic dysmenorrhoea.
2. *Congestive dysmenorrhoea*, more accurately called the premenstrual syndrome. In this group pain is a prominent symptom of their premenstrual syndrome and increases in intensity until the onset of the full menstrual flow.

Kessel and Coppen,[1] in their survey discussed in Chapter 6, conclude: "Pain was worst on the first day of the period. The other symptoms which tended to occur in the same woman were worst premenstrually. Thus there are two very common, but distinct entities – the premenstrual syndrome and dysmenorrhoea." The time, relative to menstruation, when the various symptoms were said to be worst is shown in Fig. 14.1.

There is little difficulty in the differential diagnosis.

Spasmodic dysmenorrhoea is usually acute, with colicky pains occurring at intervals of about 20 minutes, and the girl is often to be found rolling herself into a ball to obtain ease, probably with a hot water bottle on her abdomen. The pain is limited to the area of the uterine and ovarian nerve distribution, being felt in the pelvic area, the back and possibly the inner sides of the thighs. It resembles labour pains, and occasionally it may be severe enough to cause reflex vomiting or fainting. The predominant mood is one of anxiety and fear.

Many sufferers of the premenstrual syndrome, in contrast to spasmodic dysmenorrhoea, experience no pain with menstruation, and comment on the relief of their other symptoms when menstruation starts. However, if there is pain it is a continuous, heavy, dragging pain or bloatedness in the lower abdomen, increasing in severity during the premenstrual days to reach its zenith on the first day of menstruation. It may be accompanied by

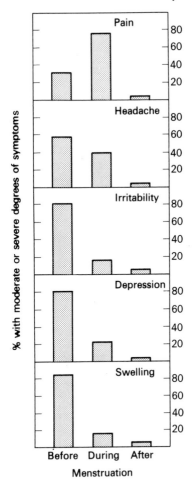

Fig. 14.1 Time of menstrual symptoms in survey of 500 women.

pains in other parts of the body, such as the breasts, head, back, and generalised pains in the joints and muscles, all characteristically accompanied by mood changes, involving depression, irritability and lethargy (Fig. 14.2).

Because spasmodic dysmenorrhoea is related to ovular cycles, pain does not accompany the first anovular cycles but usually starts a couple of years after the menarche. The first attack of dysmenorrhoea may be quite acute and unexpected owing to the previous pain-free menstruations. These painful menstruations may then alternate with painless

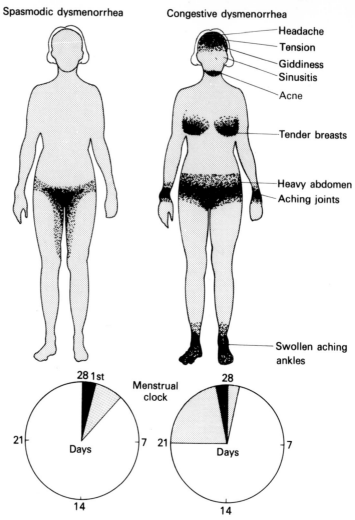

Spasmodic dysmenorrhea   Congestive dysmenorrhea

Headache
Tension
Giddiness
Sinusitis
Acne

Tender breasts

Heavy abdomen
Aching joints

Swollen aching ankles

Menstrual clock

28 1st
21
7
Days
14

28
21
7
Days
14

Fig. 14.2   Time and site of symptoms. (From *The Menstrual Cycle*, Dalton, K. Penguin Books.)

menstruation for about six months until they settled down into regular ovular cycles. The premenstrual syndrome, in contrast, is present in both ovular and anovular cycles, and indeed the regular occurrence of abdominal pain and other premenstrual symptoms may be charted even before the first menstruation.

Spasmodic dysmenorrhoea is common between the ages of 15 and 25 years, after which it usually, but not always, gradually resolves. It is relieved by dilation of the cervix and cured by a full term pregnancy. On the other hand the premenstrual syndrome may start at menarche and last until the menopause, with an increase in severity and incidence after the mid-thirties, and increase with parity.

The premenstrual syndrome increases at times of stress, while the severity of the pain in spasmodic dysmenorrhoea is unrelated to stress.

The sufferer of spasmodic dysmenorrhoea tends to be immature with small breasts, pink nipples, and scanty pubic and axillary hair. The premenstrual syndrome, however, may be found in all types of women, usually the mature woman with large breasts. Table 14.1 summarises the differences between spasmodic dysmenorrhoea and the premenstrual syndrome.

Table 14.1

Differences between Spasmodic Dysmenorrhoea and the Premenstrual Syndrome

	Spasmodic Dysmenorrhoea	*Premenstrual Syndrome*
Time of onset	Menstruation	Premenstruum
Site of pain	Uterine and ovarian nerve distribution	Lower abdomen, back, breasts, headaches, generalised joint pains
Type of pain	Spasmodic	Heavy, dragging, continuous
Age of onset	2 years after menarche	Menarche, marriage, childbirth and menopause
Predominant age group	15–25 years	Over 35 years
Effect of ovulation	Only present in ovular cycles	Present in ovular and anovular cycles
Premenstrual symptoms	Absent	Present
Effect of stress	Unrelated	Increased symptoms
Effect of pregnancy	Cures	Increases severity
Sexual development	Immature	Mature
Effect of Pill	Cures	Increases symptoms
Treatment	Oestrogens or Pill	Progesterone

Lennane and Lennane[2] have drawn attention to the fact that although spasmodic dysmenorrhoea has an obvious hormonal basis, being related to the presence of ovulation, it is too often alleged to be a psychogenic disorder. The premenstrual syndrome is likewise too often regarded as of psychogenic origin.

The importance in differentiating between spasmodic dysmenorrhoea and the premenstrual syndrome lies in the response to treatment, for spasmodic dysmenorrhoea responds readily to oestrogen, but the premenstrual syndrome responds to progesterone. The oestrogen for spasmodic dysmenorrhoea may either be administered with progestogen as an oral contraceptive pill, or alone, usually as ethinyl oestradiol in an initial dose of 50 µg from Day 5 until 25, which can be decreased in subsequent months if full relief is obtained. It is wise to continue medication for 6 to 9 months before trying the effect of a cycle without treatment.

Endometriosis with its triad of dysmenorrhoea, pelvic pain and dysparunia, may present with premenstrual symptoms. It may be suspected by the history and on vaginal examination. The diagnosis is made by laparoscopy or laparotomy. Whilst awaiting investigation such patients may usefully be started on progestogens, e.g. norethisterone 10–30 mg daily given either from Day 5 to 25, or treated continuously for several months, or with an anti-gonadotrophin, e.g. danazol, 100–200 mg three times daily.

References

1. Kessel, N., and Coppen, A. (1963), *Lancet*, **2**, 61.
2. Lennane, K., and Lennane, R. J. (1973), *New England J. Med.*, **288**, 288.

CHAPTER FIFTEEN

The Premenstrual Syndrome and Pre-eclampsia

During a survey into the incidence of the premenstrual syndrome, 192 women were personally interviewed. All had previously suffered from pre-eclampsia during the previous eight years. The record card of the pre-eclamptic pregnancy was available and the interview started by reminding the woman that during the relevant pregnancy she had been ill for two weeks (or however long her records showed). The most frequent reaction was, "No – the doctor said I was ill for two weeks, but in fact I was feeling ill throughout that pregnancy, and it was only the last two weeks that he agreed I was ill and advised me to rest." Many of these women had also experienced a normal pregnancy, either before or after the affected one, and would compare their sense of well being in a normal pregnancy with the experience of unremitting pregnancy symptoms during the pre-eclamptic one. Confirmatory evidence was in fact there on the majority of record cards, which had noted symptoms during the mid-trimester, while their blood pressure and weight gain were normal and no oedema or albuminuria observed. Some cards bore such remarks as "headaches referred to optician" or "daily vomiting – given dietary advice". The early days of pregnancy are usually accompanied by morning sickness and this is considered a natural discomfort of pregnancy, so that when the patient later mentions headache, vomiting, lethargy, irritability and depression, there is a natural tendency to assume that they are of a similar nature and therefore of little importance. Among these mothers 86% subsequently developed the premenstrual syndrome, and it was noted that the symptoms each woman had experienced during her pre-eclamptic pregnancy were the same as her present premenstrual symptoms.

Fig. 3.3 shows the symptoms the women experienced during their pre-eclamptic pregnancy and in the premenstruum.

A prospective survey into the incidence of pregnancy symptoms was then undertaken at University College Hospital, London, where 633 ante-natal patients were asked on only one occasion, between the 16th and 28th week of pregnancy, "Do you feel as well now as you did before pregnancy started?" Those who gave a negative reply were further asked about their symptoms. Their subsequent history revealed that among those who were feeling well at the time of the interview only 10% developed pre-eclampsia compared with 25% for those who had symptoms in the middle trimester. Fig. 15.1 shows that those with symptoms had a higher incidence of severe pre-eclampsia, albuminuria, stillbirths and twins. The type of pregnancy symptoms complained of are shown in Table 15.1.

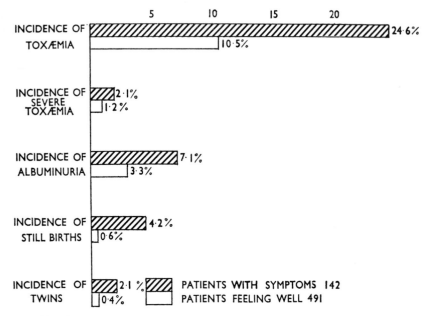

Fig. 15.1   Differences between patients with symptoms and those feeling well between the 16th and 28th week of pregnancy. (From Dalton, K. (1962), *J. Obs. and Gynaec. Brit. Commonwealth*, 69, 3.)

The similarity of premenstrual syndrome with pre-eclampsia was first noted in 1940 by Greenhill and Freed[1] who suggested the title "Toxaemia of Menstruation" as a companion to "Toxaemia of Pregnancy". As medical knowledge of the two diseases accumulates the similarity becomes more marked. Both diseases have a first stage of symptoms, either premenstrual or pregnancy, which include depression, irritability, lethargy, headache, backache, nausea and vertigo, these are present from mid-cycle or mid-pregnancy, and increase in severity as the cycle or pregnancy proceeds. This is followed by a stage of signs of oedema, weight

Table 15.1

*Pregnancy Symptom in the Middle Trimester in Women
who developed Pre-eclampsia*

Lethargy	88%
Nausea and vomiting	65%
Depression	52%
Paraesthesia	46%
Backache	44%
Headache	35%
Vertigo	26%
Fainting	12%

gain, rise in blood pressure, and albuminuria, clearly demonstrated in the
premenstrual syndrome in Figs. 5.6, 5.7 and 5.8. These symptoms may
ease with bed rest, whether in the premenstruuum or pregnancy. Finally, if
the disease progresses there is a stage of fits, either epileptic or eclamptic,
both being preceded by a severe headache, as a warning of the imminence
of a fit (Table 15.2).

Table 15.2

Similarity of Premenstrual Syndrome and Pre-eclampsia

First stage of symptoms	Nausea and vomiting
	Lethargy
	Depression
	Irritability
	Headaches
	Backache
	Fainting
	Vertigo
Second stage of signs	Weight gain
	Oedema
	Rise in blood pressure
	Albuminuria
Third stage of fits	Epileptic
	Eclamptic
	Both preceded by severe headache

In view of the similarities and the fact that premenstrual syndrome responds to progesterone if it is administered in the stage of symptoms and before the development of the stage of signs, progesterone has been used for the relief of pregnancy symptoms in the middle trimester onwards until delivery.

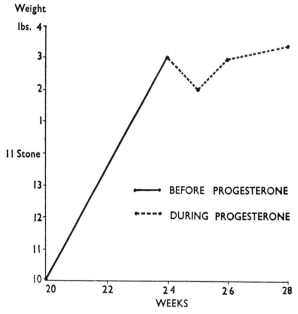

Primipara, 28 years. Oedema and heartburn at 24 weeks. Symptoms relieved by 100 mg i.m. progesterone. Maintained on 50 mg on alternate days from 24th week until normal delivery at term.

Fig. 15.2   The effect of progesterone on weight gain in pregnancy.

Fig. 15.2 shows the effect of administration of progesterone at the 24th week to a patient with pregnancy symptoms, who was showing an excessive weight gain. Initially progesterone caused a weight loss and then she had a normal pregnancy weight gain until she was delivered at term.

Progesterone Trials in the Prophylaxis of Pre-eclampsia

Controlled trials were undertaken at Chase Farm Hospital, Enfield, where women presenting with pregnancy symptoms during the middle trimester were selected at random for inclusion in the symptomatic or progesterone-treated group. In these trials the incidence of pre-eclampsia was reduced from 11% in 66 controls to 3% among 62 progesterone-treated women.

These controlled trials were later repeated at the City of London Maternity Hospital using the same protocol with similar random selection, but using progesterone suppositories or pessaries instead. The results of treatment with 400 mg progesterone suppositories or pessaries daily or thrice daily succeeded in reducing the incidence of pre-eclampsia again from 11% in 88 controls to 3% in 80 progesterone-treated women (see Table 9.1).

Progesterone Treatment

Women attending for ante-natal examination should be asked if they feel as well as before the pregnancy started, and any symptoms present should be noted on their ante-natal records. Women complaining of lethargy, nausea and vomiting, depression, pasaesthesia, backache, headache, vertigo and fainting should be given progesterone if two or more of these symptoms are present. Treatment should be started with progesterone suppositories or pessaries 400 mg b.d. or intramuscular injections of 100 mg daily for one week. When the woman returns, if there has been symptomatic relief the dose should be continued for four weeks, and then if still free from symptoms the dose may be halved and then discontinued. On the other hand if there has been no relief of symptoms the dose should be increased, using suppositories up to four times daily, or 200 mg by intramuscular injections. Progesterone should be continued as long as symptoms persist, if necessary until delivery.

Progesterone was isolated in 1934 and only three years later there were reports of clinical trials into the use of progesterone in severe pre-eclampsia, at that time only 5 mgs were injected daily for four days. With the development of progestogens in the fifties these were tried for the treatment of pre-eclampsia, until it was abruptly halted with the realisation that the administration of progestogens in early pregnancy could cause masculinisation of the female foetus. There have been no reports of masculinisation following progesterone injections, but instead there has been the encouraging finding of enhanced intelligence and educational attainments in children whose mothers benefited from progesterone (Chapter 21). There is thus every possibility that the last chapter of the Progesterone Story in relation to pre-eclampsia has not been written.

Reference

1. Greenhill, J. P., and Freed, S. C. (1940), *Endocrin.*, **26**, 529.

CHAPTER SIXTEEN

Puerperal Depression

When taking case histories from mothers with the premenstrual syndrome, it is remarkable how frequently the onset of their premenstrual syndrome follows on from a pregnancy complicated by puerperal depression. One hears such expressions as, "I've never been the same since my child was born" or, "I haven't yet got over my last pregnancy", which may have been up to ten years previously. A factory worker with severe depression stated that the onset of her illness had occurred four years previously. Later the husband was interviewed, he referred to the seven years of his wife's illness. She had two children, aged 7 and 4 years, and on both occasions had received anti-depressant drugs during the year following each birth, and the premenstrual depression had continued ever since.

In the 100 consecutive hospital cases of severe premenstrual syndrome there had been 59 pregnancies (including 6 abortions) in which puerperal depression, sufficient to need psychiatric or medical care, had occurred in 73%. Viewed from another angle, if a patient has puerperal depression, the chance of the premenstrual syndrome subsequently developing is almost 90%.

MATERNITY BLUES

Maternity Blues, defined by Pitt[2] as a mother having felt tearful and depressed in the first ten post partum days, was present in half the 100 women he studied. He concluded that it is "such a trivial, fleeting commonplace disorder that pregnant mothers should be warned to expect it to avoid being taken by surprise". It is likely that maternity blues are the result of the sudden drop in oestrogen and progesterone levels, which follows the delivery of the placenta, for by the third post partum day the hormone levels are down to those normally expected during the luteal phase of the menstrual cycle.

The maternity blues rarely last more than a few days but in about 7% to 10% of women it develops into a more serious puerperal depression, resulting not merely from the abrupt drop from the high oestrogen and progesterone levels of pregnancy, but also to difficulty in adjusting to the permanently low hormone levels of the non-pregnant state (Fig. 16.1).

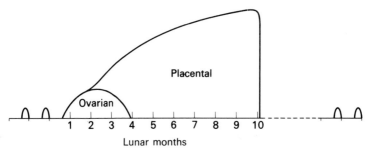

Fig. 16.1 Progesterone levels in menstruation, pregnancy and puerperium.

Lactation

Puerperal depression may have its onset quite unexpectedly when lactation ceases.

A 35-year-old professional woman with three children had experienced severe puerperal psychosis following her first two childbirths, and had received progesterone therapy for two months after the third childbirth. When her youngest daughter was eight months old she woke up one morning announcing to her husband that she "had just ovulated" although she had not had a menstruation since the pregnancy started, and had recently ceased breastfeeding. During the next few days she became increasingly depressed and so psychotic that ten days later, she needed hospital admission. Menstruation occurred normally fourteen days after the onset of her symptoms and she became normal again. She has been on progesterone treatment since for the relief of premenstrual depression and irritability.

Characteristics of Puerperal Depression

In a prospective study of puerperal depression[1] by a group of fourteen general practitioners and a psychiatrist centred on the North Middlesex Hospital, a general district hospital, the characteristics were noted to be:

1. **Favourable attitude to motherhood,** as shown by welcoming the pregnancy, being elated during pregnancy and free from pregnancy symptoms, enthusiastic about and successful at lactation.
2. **Labile emotions,** being anxious at the time of the first interview, elated during pregnancy, and then depressed during the puerperium.

Hormonal Depression

Puerperal depression has many paradoxical features. While psychiatrists often see patients who break down under the stress of a forthcoming event, such as an examination, it is rare for depressive breakdown to occur after such an event has been successfully passed and a prize has been won. Yet it would seem that it is only after nine months of discomfort and uncertainty when the longed for, healthy, baby had been born that the mother is depressed. Several surveys have stressed that puerperal depression does not occur in those who have had a previous depressive or other psychiatric illness, nor in those with a poor psychiatric, family history or childhood environment, nor does it occur in those who had many pregnancy symptoms. Even the symptoms of the puerperal depressives may differ from those found in sufferers of typical endogenous depression, for the women tend to suffer from hypersomnia rather than insomnia, and gain weight rather than lose it, they have a large appetite rather than anorexia. Nor can the hazards associated with the arrival of a new baby be blamed for causing puerperal depression, for depression does not occur in adoptive mothers, who also suffer from disturbed sleep with a crying baby demanding feeding at unearthly hours, they too have the increased responsibility for such a helpless creature and face also the divided love of the husband for the child and the wife. The evidence suggests that puerperal depression is a hormonal depression occurring in those women who have difficulty in adjusting to the abrupt alterations in the levels of progesterone after nine months of raised levels.

Progesterone Therapy

In support of the theory that puerperal depression has a hormonal aetiology is the successful treatment with progesterone. Initially progesterone should be given by injection 100 mg once to thrice daily, and when the initial symptoms have subsided the rectal or vaginal route may be used with progesterone suppositories 400 mg once or thrice daily. In view of the frequent occurrence of premenstrual syndrome after puerperal depression, progesterone therapy should be continued until menstruation returns. Once menstruation has returned, if the depression has been severe, it is wise to give treatment from Day 14 until the onset of menstruation for the next three cycles in gradually decreasing doses.

Prophylactic Treatment

In those, who give a previous history of puerperal depression or psychosis, it is worth giving up to 300 mg progesterone by injection during delivery, decreasing to 200 mg daily during the following seven days, and 100 mg daily during the second post partum week. If needed large doses can be given over the next month until the patient has really settled down. She has been used to such high doses during pregnancy that there is little danger of overdosage.

Many women who are not breastfeeding start on oral contraception shortly after delivery. If they then develop depression this may be either a true puerperal depression or one related to the side effects of the Pill, as the progestogens further lower the already low progesterone level.

With a fuller knowledge of the hormones of menstruation and pregnancy the general views on puerperal depression must change, and we will then see a transference of their treatment from the psychiatrist to the endocrinologist.

References

1. Dalton, K. (1971), *Brit. J. Psychiat.*, **118**, 689–692.
2. Pitt, B. (1973), *Brit. J. Psychiat.*, **122**, 431–433.

CHAPTER SEVENTEEN

The Outcome of Pregnancy

Pregnancy disturbs the normal rhythm of the premenstrual syndrome. At the time of the first missed menstruation the usual premenstrual symptoms become more severe and prolonged until they gradually merge into the usual symptoms of pregnancy, especially morning sickness, tiredness and the tenderness and enlargement of the breasts. Patients who are receiving progesterone for the relief of premenstrual symptoms are advised to continue with the progesterone treatment until the pregnancy is confirmed. If the symptoms have resolved, the treatment can be stopped.

After the first trimester most sufferers from the premenstrual syndrome should be free from their symptoms of asthma, migraine, epilepsy and depression and they will enjoy their pregnancy. In a small minority, however, the symptoms will persist and treatment will need to be continued to full term. It is amongst this group that the candidates for pre-eclampsia will be found (Chapter 15).

DEFECTIVE LUTEAL PHASE

Patients, in whom the basal temperature shows a rise at ovulation followed by a fall in temperature during the luteal phase, benefit from progesterone, whose thermogenic properties raise the basal temperature (Fig. 2). The progesterone should be given until a positive pregnancy test is obtained. Jones[3] has reported successful pregnancies in 12 of 15 women with this condition who were treated with progesterone suppositories.

HYPEREMESIS

In patients, who are suffering from hyperemesis of pregnancy or severe pregnancy symptoms (lethargy, irritability, depression, headache and nausea), relief may be obtained within four days by the administration of an injection of progesterone 100 mg once or twice daily and continued until the symptoms are resolved. Then a maintenance dose is required of progesterone suppositories 400 mg up to four times daily until the patient has been symptom free for about two weeks. By the 16th week the symptoms have usually subsided and by the 20th week the woman will begin to experience the feeling of well being so often associated with a normal pregnancy, or she may even feel "better than ever", free from any premenstrual symptoms and elated, this coincides with a high placental progesterone level.

SPONTANEOUS ABORTIONS

There are probably as many different causes of foetal death as in any other age group. However, there is one group of women who, having developed hyperemesis or increasingly severe pregnancy symptoms, abort spontaneously between the 8th and 14th week. Occasionally, after several weeks of daily vomiting the symptoms cease abruptly and a day or two later the woman has a spontaneous abortion, the foetus having died when the symptoms stopped.

THREATENED ABORTION

Women, who have a threatened abortion may be divided into two groups, viz. those with hyperemesis or pregnancy symptoms and those who have been free from pregnancy symptoms. In the first group of women it seems that relief of pregnancy symptoms with progesterone helps in raising the progesterone level until the placental output is adequate to maintain the pregnancy. Johansson[2] found that the mean progesterone level at the ninth week of pregnancy was significantly lower than at the fifth week (Fig. 8.2) and suggested that the placenta does not replace the corpus luteum as a major source of progesterone until about the ninth week.

A series of 24 women, who threatened to abort and had a positive pregnancy test, were treated within 12 hours of the onset of bleeding with intensive progesterone therapy sufficient to bring relief of pregnancy

Table 17.1

Progesterone Treatment of Threatened Abortion

Outcome of pregnancy	Abortion	Normal Delivery	Total
Pregnancy symptoms present	5	10	15
No pregnancy symptoms	8	1	9

Probability $= <0.01$

symptoms (Table 17.1). There was a significant difference in the outcome of the pregnancy among those 15 women with pregnancy symptoms of whom 10 (66%) had a normal delivery of a live baby, compared with the 9 women who had no pregnancy symptoms of whom only one (9%) had a normal delivery (P = < 0·01).

PROGESTERONE TREATMENT FOR HABITUAL ABORTION

Twenty-five years ago progesterone was used in patients with habitual abortion. Progesterone pellets 6 × 25 mg were implanted during the first trimester. There were conflicting reports of the efficiency of this treatment. Bishop and his colleagues claimed 86% success in those with two previous abortions and 75% with four or more previous abortions. On the other hand, Swyer and Daley, in controlled trials, found no significant difference among the treated and control patients.

Progestogens, believed to be true progesterone substitutes, then became the vogue for treatment of habitual and threatened abortion. With the realisation that progestogens produced masculinisation of the female foetus all treatment, with both progestogens or progesterone, was stopped. With our present knowledge it is obvious that the dose of progesterone used was far too small and there was no differentiation between patients with increasing hyperemesis and pregnancy symptoms, and those who were free from symptoms. Clinical experience suggests that when patients, in whom increasingly severe hyperemesis or pregnancy symptoms have preceded an abortion, are treated with progesterone during their next pregnancy, it has helped to maintain the pregnancy.

Ideally the progesterone should be administered as soon as there are pregnancy symptoms and before there is any blood loss, or threat to the foetus. I have seen many pregnancies where women, with a history of three or more spontaneous abortions, accompanied by hyperemesis or increasingly severe pregnancy symptoms, have been treated with progesterone and have gone on to full term. Among them were two women, each of whom had nine previous spontaneous abortions, they were both treated with progesterone and delivered at full term in the City of London Maternity Hospital. The use of progesterone therapy in this selected group of habitual aborters needs further assessment.

PREMATURE LABOUR

Csapa and his colleagues[1] noted that women who went into premature labour of unknown cause had a marked deficiency of progesterone and precociously increased uterine activity. They suggested progesterone treatment in such cases, adding the rider, "Can progesterone levels be increased exogenously in the third trimester when the source of progesterone is interuterinal placenta and the progesterone transport to the uterus is local rather than systemic?"

It would seem that before the potential of progesterone therapy can be fully appreciated there must be a change of attitude among those responsible for obstetric care. The expectant mother must be positively asked about pregnancy symptoms, and consideration should be given to these rather than total reliance on the presence of abnormal signs, e.g. bleeding, weight gain, hypertension or albuminuria.

PROGNOSIS OF PREMENSTRUAL SYNDROME

Three types of menstruation are found in women, those who are symptom free, and the sufferers of spasmodic dysmenorrhoea and of the premenstrual syndrome. During pregnancy, the majority of those who have symptom-free menstruation or spasmodic dysmenorrhoea will tend to have normal pregnancies, but the occasional woman will develop pre-eclampsia. On the other hand, sufferers from the premenstrual syndrome will in the main be free from their usual symptoms during pregnancy and be "better than ever", but one in ten will develop pre-eclampsia (Fig. 17.1).

During the puerperium it will be those women who were elated and "better than ever" in pregnancy who will be candidates for puerperal depression, while those who had a normal pregnancy or one complicated by pre-eclampsia may expect to feel normal during the puerperium.

When menstruation recurs after pregnancy 90% of those who suffered from pre-eclampsia or puerperal depression can expect to suffer from the premenstrual syndrome, whereas those who had a normal pregnancy may anticipate normal painfree menstruation (Fig. 17.1, overleaf). However, if progesterone has been used for the prophylaxis of pre-eclampsia or puerperal depression the chances of the premenstrual syndrome developing are diminished.

References

1. Csapa, A., Pohanka, O., and Kaihola, L. H. (1973), *Lancet*, **2**, 1097.
2. Johansson, E. D. B. (1969), *Acta. endocr. Copenh.*, **61**, 607.
3. Jones, G. S. (1973), *Le Corps J'aune* (Editors: Denamus, R., and Nelter, A.), Paris: Masson, 401–419.

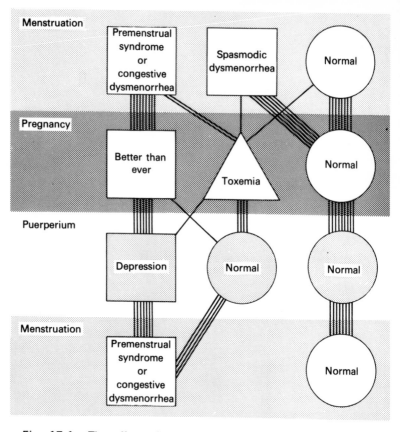

Fig. 17.1   The effect of pregnancy on menstruation. (From *The Menstrual Cycle*, Dalton, K. Penguin Books.)

CHAPTER EIGHTEEN

The Menopause

HORMONAL CHANGES

With the disappearance of the ovarian follicles and the ovarian production of oestrogen at the menopause there is an interference with the normal reproductive feedback pathways. The hypothalamus and pituitary increase their production of releasing factors and gonadotrophins to stimulate the ovaries which are no longer able to respond (Fig. 18.1). The gonadotrophin levels may show a ten-fold increase at this time, and these levels remain raised for some 16–20 years after the menopause and then gradually declines, but still remains higher than the mean values during the menstruating years.

Following bilateral oophorectomy there is an increase in plasma F.S.H. levels after six to eight days and in the plasma L.H. levels after eight to ten days. Within three weeks there is a three-fold increase in plasma F.S.H. and a two-fold increase in plasma L.H.[2]

The main oestrogen excreted from the ovary is oestradiol, but after the menopause, oestrone, a much weaker oestrogen, is synthesised in the fat, liver and other peripheral tissues from oestrogen precursors produced by the adrenals. There is no compensatory hypertrophy of the adrenals to assist in this extra production of the oestrogen precursors. After the menopause progesterone is no longer required for the proliferation of the endometrium, and as progesterone has been synthesised in the adrenals during the menstruating years there is usually sufficient to cope with the postmenopausal years. Thus the premenstrual symptoms may be expected to end two years after the last menstruation. In only a very few women cyclical symptoms continue until the mid-sixties.

Premenopausal Years

During the premenopausal years there is frequently an increase in intensity of the premenstrual syndrome, thus some find the premenstrual symptoms, which were once bearable and acceptable requiring only mild analgesia,

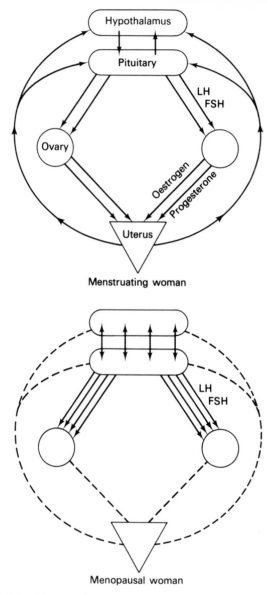

Fig. 18.1   Hormonal pathways in menstruating and menopausal women.

now become incapacitating and need medical attention. About 10% of women state that their premenstrual syndrome started at the menopause, although far more women during their early forties erroneously blame the menopause for their premenstrual syndrome.

The Last Menstruation

In Britain the mean age of the last menstruation is 49 years, with a range from 45 to 55 years. In sufferers from the premenstrual syndrome the last menstruation is likely to occur after 50 years, while those who initially suffered from spasmodic dysmenorrhoea tend to end menstruation earlier. There is a marked family similarity in the time of the menopause. In some families all the female members end early, while in others they all have a late ending. There is also a correlation between the age of menarche and that of the menopause, those starting the menarche early tend to have a late menopause.

Types of Endings

There are three common types of ending to menstruation, although any combination can occur, they are:

1. Gradual ending with decreasing loss (Fig. 18.2).
2. Missed menstruation with increasing irregularity (Fig. 18.3).
3. Abrupt ending (Fig. 18.4).

It is when there is an abrupt ending that pregnancy is feared, but vaginal examination will reveal either the warm, red, moist vagina with soft cervix characteristic of pregnancy, or the pale, dry vagina with firm cervix suggestive of the menopause. It is also the abrupt ending which is more frequently associated with depression. Often there is a possibility of the "empty nest syndrome", with the history of one or more children leaving home for employment, college or marriage. However, charting the days of depression may confirm the presence of depression during the premenstruum followed by freedom from symptoms during the postmenstrual phase, which is characteristic of premenstrual, or cyclical menopausal depression and which differentiates it from the empty nest syndrome.

Cyclical Menopausal Symptoms

For the majority of sufferers the menopause marks the end of their premenstrual syndrome; however, there is a minority in whom cyclical symptoms continue after the menopause and on into the sixties.

A 55-year-old married housewife with two children experienced a

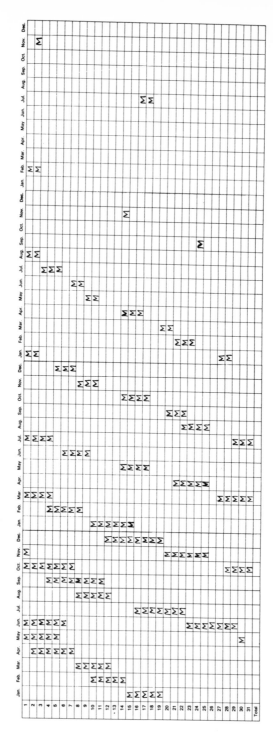

Fig. 18.2 Gradual ending of menstruation. (From *The Menstrual Cycle*, Dalton, K. Penguin Books.)

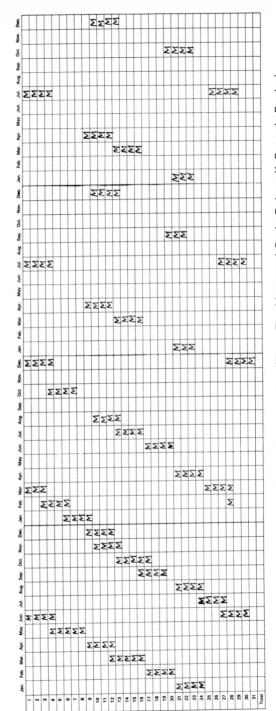

Fig. 18.3 Increasing irregularity of menstruation. (From *The Menstrual Cycle*, Dalton, K. Penguin Books.)

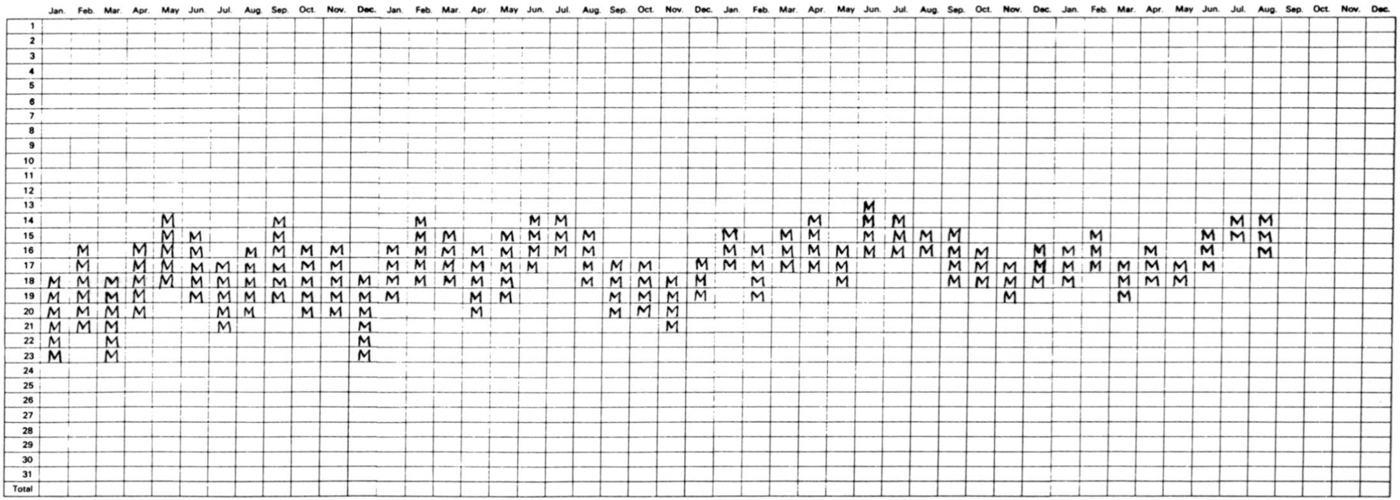

Fig. 18.4 Abrupt ending of menstruation. (From *The Menstrual Cycle*, Dalton, K. Penguin Books.)

gradual onset of periodic depression coinciding with the cessation of menstruation at the age of 47 years. She received anti-depressant drug therapy for the first two years from her general practitioner, and then was admitted to a psychiatric hospital when she developed suicidal ideas. Psychotherapy and drug therapy were of no avail, and electroconvulsive therapy brought only temporary relief, so finally at the age of 54 years she underwent a cortical undercut leucotomy. When first seen she was still severely incapacitated by her periodic depressions. The onset of an attack was preceded by a day of agitation and swelling of the face and fingers. She would then go to bed and lie staring at the ceiling all day, too apathetic to move. The attacks would last from seven to fourteen days. During her two pregnancies she had felt exceedingly well, but they had been followed by short-lived attacks of puerperal depression. The monthly rhythm of the attacks was first noticed by the husband, who stated that they were similar to, but of longer duration than, attacks of depression she had suffered with her menstruation in the days when they were courting. The husband was advised to record the days his wife spent in bed. The record of her depressed days suggested monthly cyclical attacks (Fig. 18.5), and she was treated with progesterone in gradually increasing doses. She became completely free from symptoms and was leading an active social life on treatment with progesterone injections 100 mg daily. After two years it was possible to cease treatment without a recurrence of symptoms.

Alcoholic excess is also frequent at the menopause, and in women careful observation may differentiate those whose drinking bouts only occur in association with scanty menstrual bleeding or at the time of the missed menstruation. This is a worth while differentiation, for these women can receive positive therapeutic help for an otherwise difficult and often hopeless, situation. Tragically, one husband handed in a chart, after his wife had died from an alcoholic debauch, showing seven months of cyclical attacks of alcoholism.

The increase in shoplifting in women in their fourth and fifth decades has been attributed to the cyclical depression and absentmindedness of women with this syndrome.

The commonest physical symptoms are vertigo, syncope, and rheumatic pains of the joints and muscles, the latter especially so among the obese. Water retention and obesity are common at this time, and it seems that prolonged water retention is associated with obesity.

The Effect of an Artificial Menopause
Women who have suffered discomfort and crippling symptoms during the paramenstruum will naturally look forward to the time when these

	Jan.	Feb.	Mar.	Apr.	May	Jun.	Jul.	Aug.	Sep.	Oct.	Nov.	Dec.
1									X			
2									X			
3									X			
4									X			
5								X	X			
6								X	X			
7							X	X	X	X		
8							X	X	X	X		
9							X	X	X	X		
10							X	X	X	X	X	
11							X	X	X	X	X	
12							X	X	X	X	X	
13							X			X	X	
14							X			X	X	
15							X			X	X	
16							X			X	X	
17							X			X	X	
18										X		
19										X		
20										X		
21										X		
22										X		
23										X		
24										X		
25										X		
26												
27												
28												
29												
30												
31							X					
Total												

Married Housewife, 55 years, Para 2.

X = days spent in bed, apathetic and depressed.

Fig. 18.5 Cyclical depression eight years after cessation of menstruation.

sufferings will end. Those who are advised to have a hysterectomy and/or oophorectomy know this means the end of menstruation and hope it will also relieve the attendant symptoms. Sufferers from spasmodic dysmenorrhoea and endometriosis can certainly expect relief of the pain after a hysterectomy, but sufferers from the premenstrual syndrome should be warned that they are unlikely to be relieved of their recurrent premenstrual symptoms by the operation, indeed they may well be increased in severity. As far as the premenstrual syndrome is concerned, the cyclical symptoms will recur whether or not the operation has been accompanied by bilateral oophorectomy, for the progesterone feed-back pathway will have been interrupted regardless of the presence of ovaries (Chapter 7). One surgeon is known to diagnose the premenstrual syndrome in his patients, tell them it is due to an imbalance of progesterone, perform a hysterectomy and bilateral oophorectomy and then refer them to the clinic for progesterone substitution therapy.

Cyclical Symptoms after Hysterectomy

There is frequently an interval of six to twelve months after a hysterectomy before cyclical symptoms recur, and these may be quite mild at the onset, but gradually increase in severity over the next few months. Therefore the cyclical nature of recurrent symptoms may not be obvious for a year or two.

The diagnosis of recurrent cyclical symptoms in women who have previously had an artificial menopause depends entirely upon the charting of their symptoms. It is interesting that when the patient returns with a two- or three-month record of symptoms, it is often possible to remind her of the previous length of her cycle, for a short or a long cycle is readily distinguishable. The duration of symptoms also reflects the length of previous premenstrual attacks, either drawn out and lasting for ten to fourteen days, or an acute severe one of only one or two days' duration (Fig. 18.6).

Other patients, who have had symptom-free menstruations, find that after a hysterectomy cyclical symptoms appear for the first time, as in the following patient:

A single woman working as a housekeeper. At the age of 38 years she had a hysterectomy for menorrhagia due to fibroids. After the operation she was never really well and lost 19 kg in weight. She suffered from numerous headaches, and complained of lethargy and depression. Two years later she received psychiatric treatment, which continued over the next eight years both as an in-patient and out-patient, and included drug therapy, electroconvulsive therapy and psychotherapy. When 48 years old she was referred by the psychiatrist for "chronic anxiety state and phobic symptoms which date from hysterectomy". At the interview the patient described how her attacks of depression were usually self-limiting, lasting 4 to 8 days, and accompanied by panic states, headaches and vertigo. Her chart revealed the familiar pattern of symptoms in cycles of 28 to 33 days. After her first month's treatment with progesterone the patient reported a

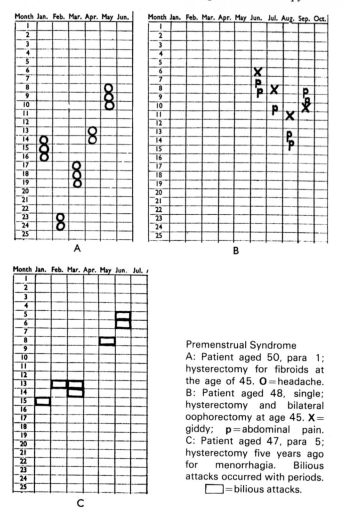

Premenstrual Syndrome
A: Patient aged 50, para 1; hysterectomy for fibroids at the age of 45. **O** = headache.
B: Patient aged 48, single; hysterectomy and bilateral oophorectomy at age 45. **X** = giddy; **p** = abdominal pain.
C: Patient aged 47, para 5; hysterectomy five years ago for menorrhagia. Bilious attacks occurred with periods.
☐ = bilious attacks.

Fig. 18.6   Cyclical symptoms after hysterectomy and oophorectomy.

gradual improvement, "feeling feminine again, working well, placid". Four months later she was completely free from symptoms, happy and anxious to tackle again her previous employment as warden of a hostel for business women, a task which called for considerable responsibility, a pleasant manner and an even temper.

The periodic attacks of lethargy, irritability and depression among sufferers make them difficult to live with, as is shown by the fact that 44% of the married women in one series of post-hysterectomy women had either divorced, separated or sought the assistance of a marriage guidance counsellor since the operation. While attacks of tension are related to menstruation the husband may be sympathetic to his marital partner, knowing that such an attack will soon end and feeling that it has an organic basis. However, after the operation the unaccountable and unexpected attacks of irritability strain the domestic harmony. As one husband put it, "She used to have a reason for it, but now she's quite unpredictable", or another, "I hoped the operation would make her more even tempered". Indeed, one remarked, "Since the hysteria operation my wife's been more hysterical than ever."

One women wrote imploring for help stating, "I had a hysterectomy two years ago, the pattern of premenstrual tension reasserted itself so that there are, as in the past, only about ten days in the month when I feel optimistic and cheerful. Since then my marriage has begun to break up and I would like at the very least to eliminate this cause of friction."

One survey of cyclical symptoms occurring after a hysterectomy showed:

Headaches	74%
Depression	62%
Vertigo	60%
Lethargy	57%
Joint and muscle pains	50%

Patients who develop symptoms after an artificial menopause are amenable to treatment. Keeping regular charts of symptoms after the operation is important for the differentiation between those whose symptoms are cyclical and therefore likely to respond to the cyclical hormone progesterone, and those whose symptoms are continuous and likely to respond best to oestrogens. Explanation of the cyclical nature of their symptoms, and the knowledge that such symptoms are likely to continue until the time of the natural menopause, helps many women to accept their symptoms. Where possible it is helpful to explain to the husband that his wife will still tend to have her monthly attacks of irritability and her "off-days".

Post Hysterectomy Depression

Two recent surveys have shown a high incidence of depression following hysterectomy,[1, 3] a finding with which most psychiatrists and general practitioners will agree. Unfortunately it is not known what proportion had cyclical depression or continuous depression, but one would suspect that many would have responded to hormone therapy with either progesterone or oestrogen. Post hysterectomy depression is most likely to occur in the following patients:

1. Under 40 years at the time of operation.
2. Previous history of depression, especially puerperal depression.
3. No gynaecological abnormality detected at operation. (In one of the surveys 45% of the uteri were reported to be normal.)
4. History of marital disruption.

Treatment of Cyclical Symptoms

Treatment of patients with cyclical symptoms, which recur at the time of missed menstruation, following either a natural or artificial menopause, respond well to progesterone. This can be administered initially by the rectal or vaginal route, and if the patient becomes free from symptoms she can have a progesterone implant, which in these circumstances usually lasts about twelve months.

Oestrogen Deficiency Symptoms

The specific symptoms of oestrogen deficiency are:

1. Hot flushes either visible or invisible, and drenching night sweats.
2. Atrophy of the vaginal epithelium, which in turn leads to pruritus and local soreness, dysparunia and loss of libido, dysuria and frequency, often misdiagnosed as "cystitis".
3. Osteoarthrosis and osteoporosis which present as generalised fleeting joint pains, especially of the feet and hands with stiffness on rising in the morning. If osteoporosis is marked there is a rise in urinary and blood calcium and in alkaline phosphatase, and later an increased incidence of fractures, especially of the wrists and neck of the femur and of crushed vertebrae.
4. Non-specific symptoms which may occur at this time and may respond to oestrogen include headaches, depression, lethargy, forgetfulness, absent-mindedness, anxiety and loss of memory.

Oestrogen Therapy

The response to oestrogen treatment in those with specific oestrogen deficiency symptoms may be dramatic, but the response of the non-specific symptoms is variable. In patients who do not respond to oestrogen therapy it may be found that their symptoms are cyclical and that they will benefit from progesterone.

Those who have been symptom-free on an oestrogen-progestogen oral contraceptive may continue on a low dosage one. Others may be given a three-week course of steroidal oestrogens, such as ethinyl oestradiol 10 to 50 μg or the conjugated equine oestrogens in doses of 0·625 to 1·25 mg daily. The non-steroidal oestrogens, such as stilboestrol, hexoestradiol and dioenestral, are best avoided as there is a remote possibility that these may prove to be carcinogenic after prolonged use. Certainly stilboestrol administered to girls in utero have been known to cause vaginal adeno-carcinomas. The aim should be to cause withdrawal bleeding at the end of the three-week course of oestrogen. If this does not follow it may be wise to add a progestogen during the last week or throughout the three-week course. Those who have had an artificial menopause can take oestrogen continuously, there is no need for three-weekly cyclical courses.

If a woman complains of headaches, bloatedness or depression when the three-week course of oestrogen is stopped it suggests either that the dose was too high, or treatment has been started too early before menopausal symptoms are present. Often such patients benefit from progesterone or progestogens for a year and then are ready for oestrogen therapy.

Contra-indications for Oestrogen Therapy

Patients in whom oestrogens are contra-indicated include:

1. Past history of coronary thrombosis or present history of angina.
2. History of deep vein thrombosis or pulmonary embolism.
3. Hormone dependent carcinoma of the breast, uterus or ovary.
4. Diabetes and liver disease.
5. Hypertension, and extra precautions are needed in those with a family history of hypertension or hypercholesterolaemia.

Progestogen Therapy

Progestogen therapy is valuable for use in those in whom oestrogen is contra-indicated, or who develop side effects on oestrogens. In these patients, the problem of progestogens lowering the blood level of proges-terone is no longer important. Progestogens are effective in stopping the flushes, preventing oesteoporosis and improving the general wellbeing. Doses of nor-ethisterone 5—10 mg may be used.

References

1. Barker, M. G. (1968), *Brit. med. J.*, **2**, 91.
2. Lauritzen, C. (1975), Estrogens in the Post-menopause. *Front. Hormone Res.*, **3**, 21–31.
3. Richards, D. H. (1973), *Lancet*, **2**, 430.

CHAPTER NINETEEN

The Sociological Significance of the Premenstrual Syndrome

World-wide evidence is slowly accumulating to show that the effects of the premenstrual syndrome are present in every aspect of a woman's life, but this does not mean in every woman's life. At times the evidence seems so universal that there is a tendency to forget that not every woman suffers to the same extent or in the same way, and that only 40–50% of the total female population are handicapped by the cyclical hormonal swings of menstruation. However, studies into the sociological effect of this syndrome are likely to become more difficult and harder to interpret in future as a larger proportion of women take the oral contraceptive pills. As explained in Chapter 8, these tend to blur the distinctive phases of the menstrual cycle and produce side effects in sufferers from the premenstrual syndrome. Already studies into sports performance in relation to menstruation, at a teacher training college in the north of England, have been abandoned as too high a proportion of the women students were on the Pill, moreover it was difficult to discern the motivation of that group of 18–20-year-olds who abstained. Were they ignorant, foolhardy or wise?

The symptom triad of premenstrual tension is depression, irritability and lethargy, and it is the presence of these symptoms that affect the behaviour and morbidity of a woman, whether she is a schoolgirl, worker, wife, mother, motorist, criminal or sportswoman.

The effect of the hormone fluctuations on young schoolgirls was shown in a study of 1,560 weekly grades of schoolgirls during one term at a boarding school. Their work was marked in some 7–12 subjects. Each grade was compared with that of the previous week and it was noticed that the standard of school work fell below the norm by 10% during the premenstrual week in comparison with a rise above the norm of 20% during the postmenstrual week. Furthermore, this pattern of premenstrual fall and postmenstrual rise was present equally in all age groups, it occurred among girls with only one menstruation per term and those who were menstruating each month, it was equally distributed among the bright girls and the duller ones, the consistent and the inconsistent worker (Fig. 19.1).

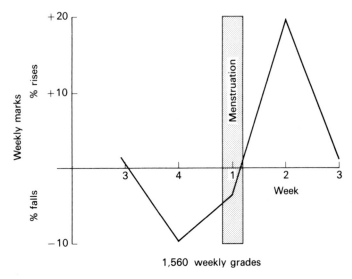

Fig. 19.1 Variation in schoolgirls' weekly grades with menstruation. (From *Brit. Med. J.* (1960), 1, 326.)

The effect of menstruation on examinations was demonstrated in respect of boarding school girls who took Ordinary ("O") level and Advanced ("A") level school leaving examinations. Those girls unfortunate enough to take examinations during their paramenstruum had fewer passes, fewer distinctions and lower average marks. It also appeared that among the 91 "O" level candidates it was those whose menstruation had a duration of six or more days who had most failures (Fig. 19.2).

Also, those girls whose menstrual cycle exceeded 31 days had more failures than the girls with shorter cycles (Fig. 19.3). The effect of the stress of these examinations in altering the girls' menstrual cycle is shown in Fig. 3.1.

These fluctuations in mental ability related to menstruation are not limited to the schoolgirl, but continue throughout the menstruating years. They may be evidenced by the typist, whose typing errors increase, by the secretary who notes down the wrong telephone number and by the actress who suddenly experiences difficulty in learning her part.

Further observations were made on boarding school girls in respect of

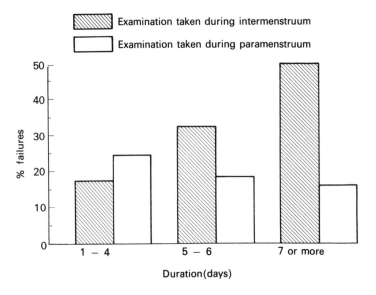

Fig. 19.2   "O" level failures and length of menstrual cycle. (From *Lancet* (1968), II, 1386.)

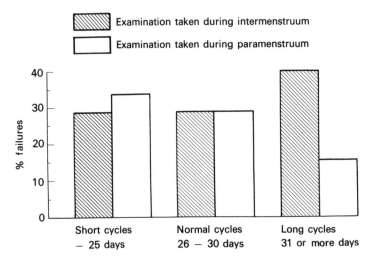

Fig. 19.3   "O" level failures and duration of menstruation. (From *Lancet* (1968), II, 1386.)

punishments. A total of 272 offences had been committed during the 14 days before, and the 14 days after the first day of menstruation. It was found that the statistically-significant figure of 29% of all offences had been committed during the first four days of menstruation, which compares with an expected incidence of 14% had there been an even distribution of offences committed during the 28 days (Fig. 19.4). The offences were forgetfulness and unpunctuality which may be attributed to lethargy.

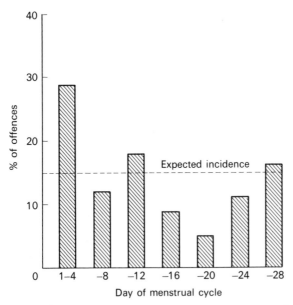

Fig. 19.4 Schoolgirls' punishments during the menstrual cycle. (From *Brit. Med. J.* (1960), **2**, 1425.)

Indeed a girl with a delayed judgement time is more likely to be punished for an offence because she was too slow to avoid detection.

Another interesting feature was that sixth form prefects aged 16–18 years, who were permitted to punish girls for misbehaviour, gave significantly more punishments during their own menstruation. Their standards of discipline tended to rise at each menstruation and then gradually fall during the cycle (Fig. 19.5). The same is true of teachers, and many a sixth form girl will watch the day-to-day irritability or calmness of her mistress to decide when it is a good moment to hand in an essay or ask a favour.

The effect of menstruation on tidiness was demonstrated in the dormitory of a London school, where each morning the 24 boarders, aged

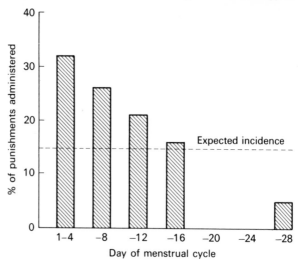

Fig. 19.5 Punishment administered by prefects during their menstrual cycle. (From *Brit. Med. J.* (1960), **2**, 1425.)

between 10 to 14 years, received a grade A to D from the Matron for the tidiness of each girl's bed and drawer. An interesting pattern was revealed, showing falls in tidiness grades occurring at intervals of 21–30 days. The dates of menstruation were unknown, except for Girl 1, it is significant that each of her three falls in tidiness grade coincided with menstruation. The question remains, was premenstrual lethargy responsible for the carelessness of the schoolgirls before breakfast? (Fig. 19.6).

A study in a woman's prison showed that among those who had committed their offence during the previous 28 days, 49% of 156 newly committed prisoners had been sentenced for crimes committed during the paramenstruum ($P = < 0.001$). The premenstrual syndrome was present in an incapacitating severity in 27% of these 156 prisoners, and it was found that 63% of these had committed their crimes during the paramenstruum, the time during which the triad of lethargy, irritability and depression was at its peak. In contrast spasmodic dysmenorrhoea (Chapter 14) was present in 14% of these prisoners, and they had committed their crimes evenly throughout the menstrual cycle. During their stay in prison those who became disorderly were reported daily to the prison governor, and here again there was a high relationship between menstruation and misbehaviour (Fig. 19.7). Indeed among those whose misbehaviour caused them to be reported more than once, 70% of offences had been committed during the paramenstruum.

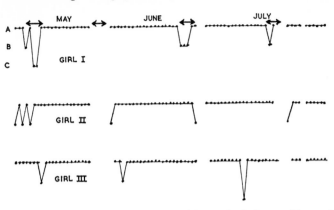

Fig. 19.6 Daily tidiness grades with cyclical drops, (From *Brit. Med. J.* (1960), **1**, 326.)

Fig. 19.7 shows the close similarity in the timing of offences committed by schoolgirls, newly-convicted prisoners and disorderly ones in relation to menstruation. The hormonal changes of menstruation render the individual less amenable to discipline, more tense, and less alert so that she

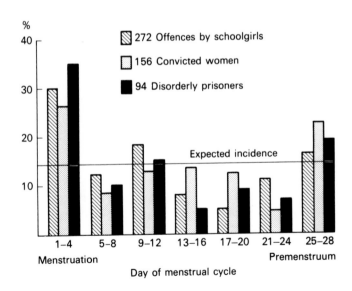

Fig. 19.7 Times of offences during menstrual cycle. (From *Brit. Med. J.* (1961), **2**, 1752.)

is more likely to be detected in her misdoings. Another aspect to be considered when schoolgirls, students and prisoners are living together in dormitories, is the possibility of menstrual synchrony occurring, which it is more likely to do when emotional experiences are shared, such as examination stress or end-of-term excitement. This tendency for their menstruations to synchronise, compounds the problems of the paramenstruum.

The cost to industry of menstruation is high. In Sweden it was estimated that 5% of absenteeism in factory, office and high school, in all communities, occurred during menstruation, while in the United Kingdom it is reckoned to be about 3% of the women at work. Among women employees using the sickbay at work 45% do so during their paramenstruum (Fig. 19.8). The effect in industry is felt most acutely where they rely heavily on female labour for their special skills, such as in the clothing trade, light engineering and assembly work. Texas Industries noted that among women employed for the assembly of electrical components a worker's normal production rate of 100 components an hour was reduced to around 75 during the paramenstruum. In the retail and distributive trades there may be a variety of effects ranging from errors in stocktaking and billing to bad-tempered service to customers and breakages from clumsiness. In the office the irritability may result in a sudden argument with the boss, the cleaner spilling her bucket of water across the room, the secretary hurling spoilt letters into the basket and a longstanding employee irrationally giving notice.

In the wards of four London teaching hospitals it was noted that 52% of admissions for accidents occurred during the paramenstruum (Fig. 19.9), a figure since confirmed by the United States Center for Safety Education, who pinpointed the 48 hours immediately before the onset of menstruation as the time when accidents are most likely to occur.

The significance of menstruation as a factor affecting accident proneness is clearly portrayed in the accidents on the road, in the home and factory and at sport; it is to be found equally among those performing routine daily tasks and those participating in unusual manœuvres. Once again one notices the increased mental and physical lethargy, the lowered judgement and increased clumsiness. The driver is liable to make irrational decisions when overtaking, she may be impatient with slow drivers, and feel aggressive towards other drivers at traffic lights. During the paramenstruum her visual acuity will be decreased and she may have more difficulty at judging distances and in doing complicated tasks such as reversing.

Social workers face an increased workload when women under their

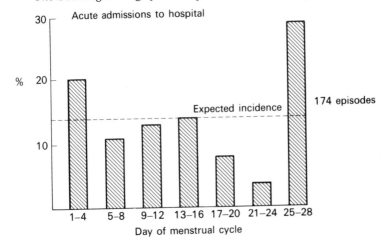

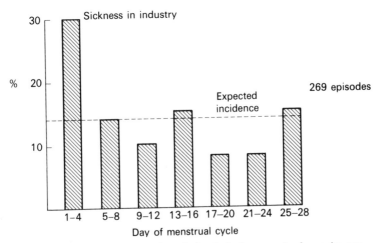

Fig. 19.8 Time of acute hospital admissions and of employees reporting sick. (From *Proceedings of the Royal Society of Medicine* (1966), **59**, 1014–1016.)

care are in the paramenstruum, for this is the time the mother is most likely to cause non-accidental injury to her children, when she may irrationally refuse entry to her home, when she is likely to quarrel with her husband, in-laws or neighbours who may report her, and when she becomes more readily intoxicated with alcohol.

The influence of menstruation on the onset of morbidity was

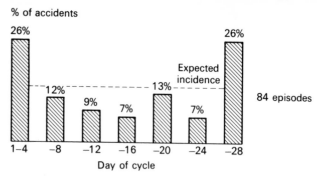

Fig. 19.9   Distribution of 84 accidents in the menstrual cycle. (From *Brit. Med. J.* (1960), **2**, 1425.)

demonstrated during an investigation carried on in the medical and surgical wards of a general hospital, and in the wards of an infectious fever hospital, when 49% of 174 acute admissions of women were found to have occurred during the paramenstruum (Fig. 19.8).

An interesting facet of the survey was the finding that viral infections tended to occur during the premenstruum, while bacterial infections predominated during menstruation. The difference may be due to the longer prodromal phase, characteristic of bacterial infection, the infection starting in the premenstruum and becoming acute during menstruation, or because bacterial infections were secondary to viral infection in the premenstruum. On the other hand, it could be related to the altered oestrogen and progesterone levels, a fact well recognised by our veterinary colleagues.

Similarly, acute admissions for psychiatric illnesses revealed that 46% of admissions occurred during the paramenstruum, indeed 53% of attempted suicides, 47% of admissions for depression and 47% of schizophrenic patients were admitted during these eight days of the cycle, findings which have since been confirmed in India and America.[1]

Even at leisure the woman is not free from the paramenstrual influence, as her partner at bridge may have discovered, or her opponent at chess or scrabble may well appreciate. Sport may be affected, and in the days before our sportswomen controlled their menstruation with hormones it was possible to foretell who would be the likely winner at tennis and other small ball sports by reference to previous performances and the effect of the premenstrual syndrome. The rise in intraocular pressure that occurs in the premenstruum affects the visual acuity. Hand and arm steadiness varies during the cycle with the unsteadiness occurring during the paramenstruum,[4] simple reaction time is not altered, but judgement and mental ability are.[2, 3] Even a slight degree of paramenstrual dyspnoea due to engorgement of the bronchial and nasal mucosa may prove a handicap in many sports.

References

1. Janowsky, D. S., Gorney, R., Castlenuovo-Tedesco, P., and Stone, C. B. (1969), *Amer. J. Obstet. Gynec.*, **Jan. 15**, 189.
2. Loucks, J., and Thompson, H. (1968), *Res. Quart.*, **39**, 2, 407.
3. Pierson, W. R., and Lockhart, A. (1963), *Brit. med. J.*, **1**, 796.
4. Zimmerman, E., and Parlee, M. B. (1973), **3**, 3, 335.

CHAPTER TWENTY

The Effect of the Premenstrual Syndrome on the Family

The linchpin of the family is the mother, so when her life becomes a misery each month, and the disturbances of the premenstrual syndrome recur, the consequences affect the whole family, the husband, infants, school-children, teenagers, and even elderly grandparents. The tragedy is that too often it continues with cyclical regularity and no one does anything about it. In its mildest form other adults should be able to joke about the premenstrual syndrome, making allowances for the temporary disturbing behaviour, but when it is severe with the symptoms causing marital stress and family suffering, specific treatment should be given.

THE YOUNG INFANT

Children and young infants of only a few months are most sensitive to mother's changes of temperament, they find it impossible to understand the mood changes and fluctuations and may react with psychosomatic problems, such as a cough, runny nose, endless crying or vomiting. In one general practice the mothers were asked to record the dates of their menstruation, and on a separate chart to record the days of their child's recurrent symptoms. After two or three months it was astonishing how many children's ailments reflected their difficulty in adjusting to the disturbances of mother's paramenstruum (Fig. 20.1). Even a 9-month girl reacted with an upper respiratory infection for three consecutive months, each one occuring during her mother's premenstruum.

A survey of 100 mothers attending surgery because their child had a cough or cold, showed that 54% of the mothers were in their para-menstruum (Fig. 20.2). The children at risk of a surgery attendance during their mother's paramenstruum were those under 2 years (71%), only children (67%), those with symptoms of less than 24 hours' duration (66%) and whose mothers were under 30 years (63%).

	Jan.	Feb.	Mar.	Apr.	May	Jun.
1						
2						
3						
4						
5						
6						
7						
8						
9					X	
10					X	
11					X	
12					X	
13					XM	
14				X	XM	
15				X	XM	
16				X	M	
17				X		
18				MX		
19		X			M	
20		X			M	
21		X	X		M	
22	X	MX	X		M	
23	X	MX	M			
24	X	M	M			
25	MX	M	M			
26	MX		M			
27	M					
28	M					
29						
30						
31						
Total						

M = mother's menstruation

X = child's colds

Male child 2 years 4 months.

Fig. 20.1   Relationship of a child's colds to mother's menstruation.

There was a possibility that the general practice was biased, so the survey was repeated at the North Middlesex Hospital, a general district hospital, questioning the mothers of 100 children who had been admitted as an emergency. The result was similar; whether the admission was for an accident or an illness, 49% of the mothers were in their paramenstruum at the time of their child's admission (Fig. 20.3). Of course, if the mother is accident prone during her paramenstruum, her action may either result in

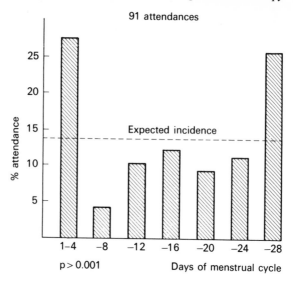

Fig. 20.2 Surgery attendance of mothers with sick children. (From *The Menstrual Cycle*, Dalton, K. Penguin Books.)

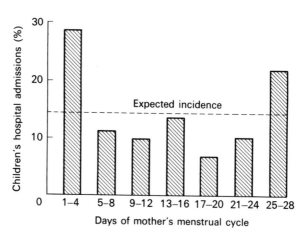

Fig. 20.3 Children's hospital admissions and mother's menstruation. (From *Lancet* (1968), II, 1386.)

an accident to herself or her child, for example, if she is pouring out the tea and spills it, the boiling tea may either scald her or her child, if he is standing too near.

Sibling Jealousy Misdiagnosed

It is easy to diagnose "sibling jealousy" in an older child, who has only displayed symptoms of temper tantrums, enuresis or recurrent abdominal pain since the birth of a younger sibling, but there may be another explanation. Premenstrual syndrome tends to increase in severity with age and parity, especially if the pregnancy had been complicated by pre-eclamptic toxaemia or puerperal depression.

A 30-year-old mother, had been "better than ever" during her second pregnancy. She would take David, aged 3 years, each afternoon to play on the swings or kick a football in the recreation grounds. However, following an easy labour and the delivery of a much-wanted daughter, she became severely depressed, needing psychiatric help. During the following year David, who had been dry, developed enuresis again. Of course his sister was inevitably blamed until a chart (Fig. 20.4) showed that his bedwetting nights coincided with his mother's premenstruum. She then admitted that during the premenstruum she became too lethargic to play football or take unnecessary walks in the park and possibly even to attend to his toilet before bedtime; also her breasts became tender and she spent her time fending him off when he wanted a good hug. Treatment of mother's premenstrual syndrome ended David's enuresis.

Non-Accidental Injury

The most tragic presentation of premenstrual syndrome is when the mother has a sudden aggressive outburst and in an irrational hysterical attack batters her baby. When non-accidental injury is suspected in an apparently loving mother one of the most important questions to ask is the date of her last menstruation.

A social worker's report on a 35-year-old mother of two children read:

"During the last premenstruum her youngest daughter, aged 18 months was screaming and would not stop. Patient was very irritated by this and picked her up and squeezed her – this started a circle of louder screaming and a harder squeezing until patient 'heard something crack'. She was immediately frightened and threw the child on the floor and sat crying on a chair. When more composed she examined Joan and took her to the doctor."

A 27-year-old housewife explained, "I was teaching my five year old daughter to weave – she wasn't attending – she kept looking out of the window – I shouted at her – she started trembling – then I couldn't help it I

	Jul.	Aug.	Sep.	Oct.	Nov.	Dec.
1						
2					X	
3					M	
4					M	
5				X	M	
6					M	
7				X	M	
8					M	
9				M		
10				M		
11				M		
12				M		
13				M		
14			X	M		
15			M	M		
16			M			
17			M			
18			M			
19			M			
20		X	M			
21			M			
22		M	M			
23		M				
24		M				
25		M				
26		M				
27		M				
28		M				
29		M				
30						
31						
Total						

M = Mother's menstruation
X = Child's enuresis

Fig. 20.4   Enuresis chart and mother's menstruation.

hit her good and truly. It was only afterwards I realised I had started menstruating."

Both these cases were treated with progesterone and their aggression ceased.

The Schoolchild

When the child goes to school it may be obvious to teachers from a glance at the lateness register or absentee list that the mother is having monthly difficulties. School doctors should be informed of such warning signs. It was noticed that a 10-year-old girl's name repeatedly appeared on the absent list at the beginning of each month. When the mother attended a few days later it transpired that she had recurrent asthma which necessitated bed rest and the daughter was kept at home to answer the door. How much better to treat the mother's premenstrual asthma rather than let the child's education suffer.

On a mother's lethargic premenstrual days she is liable to send the children off on errands, and then scold them for buying items which are too expensive, or for getting the wrong change. She may be too tired to attend school concerts or parent's evenings, when they occur in the paramenstruum.

Teenagers' Problems

Unfortunately, for many families, due to the average age differences, the teenage years of the children coincide with a worsening of the premenstrual syndrome during the premenopausal phase of the mother. When premenstrual tension gets worse teenagers find it difficult to make contact with mother, never being sure of her reaction beforehand, or they may turn aside with the comment, "She's in one of her moods – don't ask her today."

Daughters are more likely to understand the mood changes and may indeed have personal experience. It is important to discuss the problem openly with teenagers of both sexes, explaining to them that many of the quarrels with their friends and their unexpected tears may well be due to the changes in hormonal levels.

With mother and daughter living closely together there is the possibility of menstrual synchrony occurring, so exacerbating any disharmony in the household during the paramenstruum. One mother wrote about her daughter who was receiving treatment for premenstrual irritability and food cravings. "Some cakes and biscuits disappeared on Sunday. It was all too much for me and I burst in tears. This in turn upset my husband, who went and found Mary in her bedroom and gave her a good thrashing. At midnight we discovered she was missing. She had spent the night with friends." Both mother and daughter started menstruating that same day.

The Grandparents

The elderly grandparents may also be the butt of their daughter's jaded premenstrual moods, at which time continual complaints are made of their eating and sleeping habits, or failure to follow simple instructions. In general practice the doctor watches as the elderly parent gradually becomes more senile and helpless, and stands by ready to offer all his help and the social services as they are needed. But it is interesting how suddenly, and it is always suddenly and with great urgency, that the request is made for the elderly relative to be moved away. The daughter can no longer cope – it is all too much for her. At great length and in the finest detail she will tell of all the difficulties. If at this moment it is possible to ask her, it is usual to find that the caring relative is in her paramenstruum and her ability to care and to love has temporarily disappeared, although it will return in the postmenstruum. More than one husband has arranged for help in the home for one week each month, rather than one day each week, in order to prepare for the difficulties of the paramenstruum.

The Husband

The wise husband knows that when his wife wakes up "a changed personality" it is one of those days when he must treat her with care or else her irrational wrath will burst upon him.

To be married to a sufferer of severe premenstrual syndrome calls forth qualities of understanding, flexibility and leadership. The husband needs to be aware of the fluctuations of mood during the paramenstruum and have confidence that normality will be resumed once the postmenstruum is reached. He needs to be ready to step into the breach and assume control at awkward moments. Most of all he must realise that stress will increase the severity of her symptoms and also that long spells without food may have disastrous consequences and can always be avoided.

One survey showed that the husband's late arrival at work was a reflection of the time of his wife's cycle. They both failed to get up with the alarm, they quarrelled over breakfast which consequently took longer, and then the sandwiches weren't ready!

A door to door salesman was referred for treatment after his employers noticed that one week in four his sales record was abysmal and his commission practically nil. By consultation with his wife's diary it became apparent that the bad weeks corresponded in each instance with his wife's paramenstruum. During the interview the husband spoke of his wife's changed personality on those days, how she became "impatient and dogmatic". When she had received progesterone treatment, the husband returned saying she was now "like the woman I married".

One husband realised that if they discussed their household budget and possible economies during the paramenstruum no agreement could be reached. He solved the problem by asking the bank manager to send the statements at carefully chosen dates when his wife was in her postmenstruum and would be reasonable and amenable to suggestions.

Henderson of Melbourne has shown that the husband's basal temperature curve is related to that of his wife, and that both have a characteristic ovulation drop followed by a rise in temperature, although this does not occur when the woman is on the Pill, nor among males living alone.

The young child is the most sensitive barometer of the approaching storms and tempests, foreshadowed by the mother's premenstrual pattern. The husband and older children come next and it is important that their ability to diagnose the condition is used to the full. Doctors should always be ready to listen to the husband's story.

CHAPTER TWENTY-ONE

A Glimpse of the Future

By now the influence of the premenstrual syndrome on every aspect of a woman's life and its resolution with progesterone therapy will be fully appreciated. It is also hoped that the misconceptions regarding progesterone and progestogens have been clarified. So far the negative side of the premenstrual syndrome has dominated the scene. It is now time for the positive aspect, the postmenstrual peak to take the field, for this surely is that attainable norm for all women. As a consequence of progesterone therapy, many more women are now enjoying trouble-free menstrual cycles and experiencing as a norm what was once their postmenstrual peak. By resolving the hazards of the paramenstruum the sociological consequences have been nullified and the economic losses of time off work, disruption and wastage greatly reduced.

The similarity of the premenstrual symptoms to those of early pregnancy and their treatment with progesterone has been shown to reduce the incidence of pre-eclampsia from 11% to 3% in those hospitals where it has been used. This, too, has produced a bonus in the freeing of ante-natal beds.

As yet it is only a privileged few who are able to obtain these benefits of progesterone therapy. It is now time for these to be enjoyed by all who are in need of treatment. The diagnosis and treatment of the premenstrual syndrome is within the capabilities of every general practitioner, whilst every physician, endocrinologist, gynaecologist and psychiatrist should be aware of his responsibilities for the diagnosis and treatment of such presentations as come within his field. The cost of progesterone is high, but it can be prescribed under the National Health Service. Moreover, as long ago as 1958 the tribunal on over-prescribing ruled that progesterone was a "reasonable and necessary" treatment for patients with the premenstrual syndrome. When the cost is weighed against the sociological and economic effects described in the last two chapters it is negligible.

There is one apparently very special property of progesterone that has still to be mentioned. When progesterone has been administered to the pregnant mother, the child of that pregnancy appears to possess enhanced intelligence and educational attainment. Attention was focused on this possibility by a chance remark: "How curious that so many of your patients are among the brightest at the local school." Looking at the ante-natal records of the mothers of these children it was noted that all had received progesterone for pregnancy symptoms during that pregnancy. A simple pilot study was arranged by the local medical officer and the results were encouraging. Later examination by community physicians and health visitors at the first birthday of progesterone children and controls, born at the Chase Farm Hospital during the controlled trials into the prophylactic value of progesterone in the treatment of pre-eclampsia, provided further evidence of earlier standing and walking among progesterone children (Fig. 21.1).

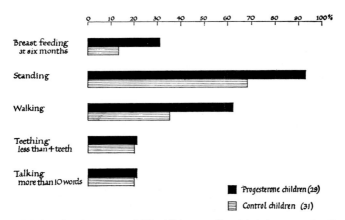

Fig. 21.1   Attainments of 60 children at first birthday examination. (From *Brit. J. Psych.* (1968), 516, 114, 1377.)

A follow-up at the City of London Maternity Hospital was then organised in which each progesterone child was matched with the next born normal control child and with a child whose mother had developed pre-eclampsia, using the labour ward register. The children were then 9–10 years old and unknown to the author. Their respective head teachers were asked to assess the named child's ability as "average", "above" or "below" in English, verbal reasoning, arithmetic, craft work and physical education (Fig. 21.2).

The results showed an increased number of progesterone children were regarded as above average in the academic subjects, English, verbal reasoning and arithmetic.

Furthermore, among the progesterone children the results were dose

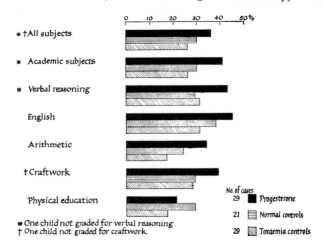

Fig. 21.2   Above average school grades of 79 children at 9–10 years. (From *Brit. J. Psych.* (1968), 516, 114, 1377.)

dependent, being best among those in whom administration began before the 16th week (Fig. 21.3), and with a dose exceeding 8 g (Fig. 21.4).

A follow-up of these children, now 18 to 20 years, shows that more progesterone children stayed at school longer, obtaining more "O" levels and "A" levels and 11 (32%) of the 34 progesterone children obtained

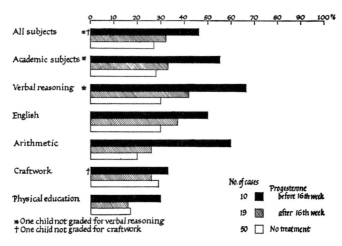

Fig. 21.3   Above average school grades and time of progesterone administration. (From *Brit. J. Psych.* (1968), 516, 114, 1377.)

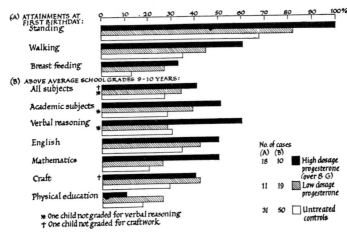

Fig. 21.4 Effect of high dosage progesterone on attainments. (From *Brit. J. Psych.* (1968), 516, 114, 1377.)

university places compared with 6% of controls, 6% of children in the borough of Haringey, in which most of the children lived, and 6% for the Inner London Education Authority. Again, the effect of the progesterone was dose dependent, being best when administered early in high doses for longer than 8 weeks.[2]

Two psychologists from Stanford University[3] gave a full two-hour testing to thirty of these progesterone children and concluded that there was a clear advantage in the Differential Aptitude Test in numerical ability and marginally significant relationship with spatial and mechanical ability in relation to the dose of progesterone received. The Bem sex-role inventory and the Californian Psychological Inventory did not relate significantly with masculinity or feminity score.

This is only a beginning, but it is a field in which considerably more work needs to be done, not only to confirm or refute these findings but to provide a greater understanding of the mechanism of action of progesterone in the human and the role it plays in the evolution of life. In this chapter the veil has been lifted slightly to give a tantalising glimpse of what may be possible for the next generation, but we have come a long way from our original starting point of Hippocrates and "the agitated blood of the womb seeking a way of escape from the body". It is now time for us to come down from the dizzy heights of speculation to the workaday world that awaits us on the other side of the surgery door, where suffering women are awaiting our attention in the diagnosis and treatment of their premenstrual symptoms.

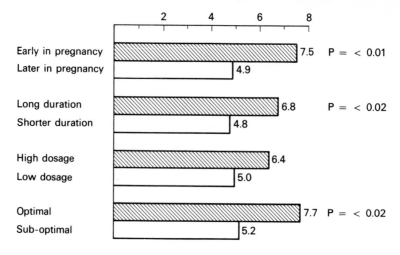

Fig. 21.5   Effect of progesterone dosage on "O" levels.

References

1. Dalton, K. (1968), *Brit. J. Psych.*, **516**, 114–1377.
2. Dalton, K. (1976), *Brit. J. Psych.*, **129**, 438–442.
3. Zussman, J. U., Zussman, P. P., and Dalton, K. (1975), *Soc. Red. Child Devel. Denver* (awaiting publication).

THE BRITISH SCHOOL OF OSTEOPATHY
1-4 SUFFOLK STREET, LONDON SW1Y 4HG
TEL: 01-930 9254-8

Author's Publications

"The Premenstrual Syndrome" (1953), Joint authorship R. Greene. *Brit. med. J.*, **1**, 1007.

"Similarity of Symptomotology of Premenstrual Syndrome and Toxaemia of Pregnancy and their Response to Progesterone" (Charles Oliver Hawthorne B.M.A. Prize Essay – 1954), ibid., **2**, 1071.

"The Premenstrual Syndrome" (1955), *Proceedings of the Royal Society of Medicine*, **48**, 5, 337.

"The Aftermath of Hysterectomy and Oopherectomy" (1957), ibid., **50**, 6, 415.

"Toxaemia of Pregnancy Treated with Progesterone During the Symptomatic Stage" (1957), *Brit. med. J.*, **2**, 378.

"Menstruation and Acute Psychiatric Illnesses" (1959), ibid., 1, 148.

"Comparative Trials of New Oral Progestogenic Compounds in the Treatment of the Premenstrual Syndrome" (1959), ibid., **2**, 1307.

"Effect of Menstruation on Schoolgirls' Weekly Work" (1960), ibid., **1**, 326.

"Schoolgirls' Behaviour and Menstruation" (1960), ibid., **2**, 1647.

"Menstruation and Accidents" (1960), ibid., **2**, 1425.

"Early Symptoms of Pre-eclamptic Toxaemia" (1960), *Lancet*, **1**, 198.

"Menstruation and Crime" (1961), *Brit. med. J.*, **2**, 1752

"Controlled Trials in the Prophylactic Value of Progesterone in the Treatment of Pre-eclamptic Toxaemia" (1962), *J. Obstet. Gynaec. Brit. Comm.*, **69**, 3.

"The Present Position of Progestational Steroids in the Treatment of Premenstrual Syndrome" (1963), *Medical Woman's Federation*, July, 137.

"The Influence of Menstruation on Health and Disease" (1964), *Proc. roy. Soc. Med.*, **57**, 4, 262.

"The Premenstrual Syndrome" (1964), London: William Heinemann Medical Books. Translated into Spanish.

"The Influence of Mother's Menstruation on her Child" (1966) (Charles Oliver Hawthorne, B.M.A. Prize Essay), *Proc. roy. Soc. Med.*, **59**, 10, 1014.

"The Influence of Menstruation on Glaucoma" (1967) (Charles Oliver Hawthorne, B.M.A. Prize Essay), *Brit. J. Ophthal.*, **51**, 10, 692.

"Ante-Natal Progesterone and Intelligence" (1968), *Brit. J. Psych.*, **516**, 114, 1377.

"Menstruation and Examinations" (1968), *Lancet*, **11**, 1386.

"The Menstrual Cycle" (1969), Penguin Books. Translated into eight languages.

"Children's Hospital Admissions and Mother's Menstruation" (1970), *Brit. med. J.*, **2**, 27–28.

"Prospective Study into Puerperal Depression" (1971), *Brit. J. Psych.*, Vol. 118, N. 547.

"Premenstrual and Puerperal Depression" (1971), *Proc. Roy. Soc. Med.*, **64**, 12, 1249–1252.

"Progesterone Suppositories and Pessaries in the Treatment of Menstrual Migraine" (1973), *Headache*, **12**, 4, 151.

"Migraine – A Personal View" (1973), *Proc. roy. Soc. Med.*, **66**, 3, 263–266ff (Section of General Practice, pp. 21–24.)

"Migraine in General Practice" (Migraine Trust Prize Essay) (1973), *J. Roy. Coll. Gen. Pract.*, **23**, 97.

"Effect of Progesterone on Brain Function" (1975), *X Acta Endocrin. congr.*, Amsterdam.

"The Progesterone Story" (1975), *Symposium of Psychosomatic, Puberty and Gynaecology*, Vienna.

"Food Intake Prior to a Migraine Attack – Study of 2,313 Spontaneous Attacks" (1975), *Headache*, **15**, 3, 188–193.

"Bromocriptine in Premenstrual Syndrome" (1976), *Symposium Bromocriptine*, Royal College of Physicians, London.

"Menstruation and Sport" (1976), Chapter in *Sports Medicine*, 2nd edition (edited by J. G. P. Williams and P. N. Sperrin), London: Edward Arnold.

"Sexual and Menstrual Problems in the Blind" (1976), Conference of Sexual Problems of the Disabled. Royal College of Obstetricians and Gynaecologists, London.

"Migraine and Oral Contraceptives" (1976), *Headache*, **15**, 4, 247.

"Clinician's View of the Menopause" (1976), *Roy. Soc. Health J.*, **96**, 2, 75–77.

"Prenatal Progesterone and Educational Attainments" (Charles Oliver Hawthorne Prize 1976), *Brit. J. Psych.*, November, **129**, 438.

Index